PEACE-MAKERS

Christian Voices from the New Abolitionist Movement

Jim Wallis, editor

WITHDRAWN

1817

HARPER & ROW, PUBLISHERS, San Francisco
Cambridge, Hagerstown, New York, Philadelphia,
London, Mexico City, São Paulo, Sydney

To Charles Finney and the other abolitionists of the nineteenth century who, by the grace of God, persevered in faith and saw their vision become a reality.

FIRST EDITION

Library of Congress Cataloging in Publication Data
Main entry under title:

PEACEMAKERS, CHRISTIAN VOICES FROM THE NEW ABOLITIONIST MOVEMENT.

    1. Atomic warfare—Religious aspects—Christianity—Addresses, essays, lectures. 2. Peace—Addresses, essays, lectures. I. Wallis, Jim.
BR115.A85P35 1983   261.8′73   82–48940
ISBN 0–06–069244–8

---

83 84 85 86 87 10 9 8 7 6 5 4 3 2

PEACEMAKERS

Acknowledgments

Thanks for this book go to all the authors who contributed their time and their stories to *Peacemakers*. It is their testimonies, and those of the multitude of Christians they represent, that are our greatest sign of hope in a nuclear age.

Special thanks go to Lindsay McLaughlin, who assisted with the editing on this project from beginning to end. This book, along with most other books I have done, could not have been pulled together without Lindsay's competent help and encouraging spirit. The hope for a more peaceful world for our children expressed in *Peacemakers* became even more significant during the editing as Lindsay and her husband, Billy, learned they were pregnant with their first child.

Thanks go to Susan Masters as well, who patiently typed the manuscript.

Introduction

I was born in 1948, part of the postwar baby boom. I first learned of the bomb through my father, who had been a Navy lieutenant scheduled to be part of the force for the invasion of Japan: he told us that it had saved his life.

None of us would have been here, I figured, had it not been for the atomic bomb. I remember being grateful that our family had been given a chance to come into being. I felt some pride, too, at our country's great technological and scientific achievement in being the first to create such an awesome weapon.

I was never told anything about what the bomb did to the people of Hiroshima and Nagasaki. I only knew that it had ended the war and brought my father home. I didn't once think about the Japanese. Anyway, "the Japs" had bombed Pearl Harbor, hadn't they? They started it.

I never gave the bomb another thought until a high school teacher assigned me a book to read, *Hiroshima* by John Hersey.

I was shocked and stunned. The book was simply an account of what happened to Hiroshima and its people on August 6, 1945. Hersey's vivid portrayal of the bomb's destruction and devastation was not overly dramatic or emotional. It didn't have to be. For the first time, I read the story of the people who had suffered the world's first atomic explosion. Drawn from the testimony of eyewitnesses and survivors, *Hiroshima* graphically tells of the horror suffered by the innocent families who experienced the hell of that dread day.

The world had never before seen such a thing. And I never imagined anything like it. For the first time, I saw the atomic bombing through the eyes of its victims. Our enemies had human faces. They cried in their pain and agony just as we would have. I had never before heard, even in the church, the story told from the perspective of the victims, though that is always the most biblical perspective.

My father had come home safely, but at what cost of human suffering, agony, and grief? Why hadn't I been told about this before? I remember arguing with my father over whether the bomb had really been necessary.

I wondered how many bombs like that dropped on Hiroshima existed in the world. When I learned the number, I was deeply concerned. Hiroshima had started something that had gotten out of control. Quietly, and with little public attention or outcry, the United States and the Soviet Union were amassing nuclear arsenals unprecedented in their destructive capacity. I wondered where the world was heading. To end a war and save my family, something had been begun that now threatened the whole world and all its families, including my own. The destruction I had read about in Hiroshima had seared my conscience, but that devastation would be small compared to what would happen if the bomb were used again.

Later I read Thomas Merton, who wrote that to defeat Hitler, we had become like him. The victory of Nazism, said Merton, was present in the ashes of Hiroshima and Nagasaki. With the advent of nuclear weapons and the expressed willingness of the superpowers to use them, the world was becoming more and more like the one envisioned by Hitler. Once we consented to risk global holocaust, other acts of violence against human life became increasingly permissible.

My study of history during university years showed that the Japanese had been near surrender before the atomic bomb was dropped. The entire country had been heavily carpet-bombed, though the cities of Hiroshima and Nagasaki had been spared, making them "virgin territory" on which to demonstrate the power of the new weapon. Proposals that a demonstration bomb be dropped on an uninhabited island as a threat and warning were rejected. Only three days after Hiroshima, before the Japanese had had time to realize fully what had happened, the second bomb destroyed Nagasaki. That unnecessary act of cruelty compounded the shame of Hiroshima.

Many historians and political commentators now say that the real purpose in dropping the atom bomb was to make a show of strength to the Russians. The Soviets needed to be intimidated and made afraid of American power. A demonstration of the bomb's destructive capacity would establish American military superiority and enable the United States to exercise more influence after the war.

In the postwar world, however, the United States couldn't produce enough atom bombs soon enough to dictate terms, and the Soviets quickly developed their own atom bomb. The nuclear arms race had begun, launched on the broken bodies and smoldering ruins of Hiroshima and Nagasaki. Since 1945 the arms race has been central to the competition between the United States and the Soviet Union for global influence.

The bomb was developed in secret. Similarly, United States nuclear policy has never been the subject of national political debate. The most important questions affecting the life of every American—and of everyone in the world for that matter—have been decided by a handful of political rulers, without discussion or consent of the people. In recent times we have seen revelations that American policy-makers have considered using nuclear weapons on a number of occasions—sometimes against nonnuclear powers, as when the U.S. government contemplated using nuclear weapons in Korea and Vietnam. On this most crucial issue that overrides all others, the American people have never had any influence or voice.

The crisis of nuclear weapons has become very personal for me and for Sojourners community. For years now, the nuclear danger has preoccupied our minds, hearts, prayers, and actions. The labor for peace has been long and often hard, involving speaking, writing, vigiling, demonstrating, organizing, resisting war taxes, committing civil disobedience, going to jail. For all in our community, the nuclear arms race has been a point of conversion. Our struggle for peace has deepened our faith and reshaped our lives.

From the beginning, we have seen nuclear weapons as not only a threat to survival, but as a crisis of faith. Our acceptance of these weapons among us poses a theological and spiritual challenge, not just a political problem. We have held that the church's response to the nuclear danger will be the most urgent test of our conversion in this perilous age.

Others objected at first. This was a military problem, they said, a political policy question rather than a religious one. The church should not venture into so complex an area as nuclear strategy and military policy. No, we insisted, if the church does not intrude into the moral paralysis with a clear and unequivocal no to nuclear weapons, the gospel will have no meaning for our time. The nuclear crisis has become for us a matter of faith. In fact, we see it as the most serious test of faith in the 1980s.

With nuclear weapons, the clear moral choice that has emerged supersedes all complex argumentation. The existence and proliferation of nuclear weapons has become for us what slavery became for many Christians in the nineteenth century. The parallel between nuclear weapons and slavery was, for us, natural, and we made the connection early. Perhaps we were helped by our evangelical heritage and tradition. As a preacher, I had learned that sin must be attacked clearly and publicly and the salvation available in Christ made concrete to each and every age. Never was the gospel of peace more needed.

We took great strength and courage from the abolitionists of the last century. Their burning faith and tireless commitment against slavery created a spiritual force that eventually toppled that hideous institution. At first abolitionists were thought to be idealists, utopian dreamers, and even fools. Who could imagine a world without slavery? The whole economy, it was said, rested upon it. But the revivalists who traveled the length and breadth of this country would not be satisfied with mere reform and moderate improvements. They demanded nothing less than the total abolition of slavery. It took decades of perseverance, sacrifice, and suffering. A world without slavery could only be seen, at first, through the eyes of faith. But because of the abolitionists' clear and unrelenting vision, others also came to see. Through faith, prayer, sweat, blood, and tears, a new day of freedom and justice was born.

Our situation today is even more perilous and threatening. We have less and less time. The nuclear spring is being wound tighter and tighter each day. The struggle for peace will be at least as arduous and costly as the battle against slavery, and probably more so. The stakes have never been greater. But the testimony of the abolitionists remains as the hopeful story of how a vision of faith became a reality.

Today a revival of faith that brings spiritual transformation is the best hope of ending the arms race and abolishing nuclear weapons. That revival has already begun, and its key is the recognition of the nuclear crisis as a spiritual crisis. The nuclear danger is becoming an occasion of fresh conversion for growing numbers of Christians as opposition to nuclear weapons is seen as a matter of obedience to Jesus Christ. A "new abolitionist movement" is emerging based on prayer, preaching, commitment, and sacrifice. This conversion of whole sectors of the church to peace is unprecedented and is the most visible sign of spiritual renewal in our day.

The prophets among us saw the spiritual implications of the nuclear question and alerted the rest of the church. Now church leaders are taking stands that put them in direct opposition to our government's policy. Whole churches and congregations are becoming active peacemakers. Ordinary Christians are making life-changing decisions for the sake of peace. The God of the Bible is being rediscovered as the Author of Life, and God's Son as the Prince of Peace. The moral contradiction of spending billions of dollars to prepare for global holocaust while people go hungry is being exposed as the sin that it is.

I believe that only the church can stop the arms race now. Without the consent and support of the Christian community the arms race could not continue. Our greatest political hope is for the churches of East and West to regain the biblical vision of the body of Christ, which knows no boundaries of race, nation, or ideology but lives in the world as a community of reconciliation.

The people of God could unite to create the moral force to stop the insanity of the world's political wisdom, leading the way to peace. Christians could refuse to cooperate with our nation's nuclear policies, obstruct war-making plans, and point to alternatives for real security.

But the way to peace will be the way of the cross for those who choose to be peacemakers. It was for Jesus, and it will be for all those who follow his path. If the churches are to provide leadership for peace, they will certainly rediscover the cross. No longer an ancient relic or piece of religious symbolism in our church sanctuaries, the cross will once again become the sign of our lives.

Political realists and media commentators cannot imagine a world without nuclear weapons. Only those with the eyes of faith will be able to see it. But if those who do will persevere like their abolitionist forbears, many others will eventually come to see the way to a world free of the nuclear scourge.

This book is a sign of that hope. Here are Christians who are being converted because of nuclear weapons. Their testimony speaks for the millions more who are also rediscovering Christ's way of peace. They come from across the entire spectrum of the church's life, yet they speak with one voice—an urgent plea for peace.

Such a collection of Christian voices is itself an important ecumenical event. The urgency of the historical situation and the movement of God's Spirit brings them together. They and the growing multitude they represent are the beginning of the new abolitionist movement.

Our great hope is that the full spiritual resources of the church will be brought to bear on the world's desperate struggle for life. We pray as one that the power of God might flow through our lives so that the power of the bomb might be broken forever.

Janet and Robert Aldridge
A Nuclear Engineer's Family

In 1956 Lockheed Aircraft Corporation moved its missile division to the San Francisco Bay Area. The plant they built in Sunnyvale was later to become Lockheed Missiles and Space Company. Wanting to get back into aeronautics, Bob hired on in the engineering department and we bought our present home in Santa Clara. Our sixth and youngest child was not quite a year old at the time.

Before we accepted work at Lockheed, and before we moved to the Bay Area, we did some serious thinking about the function of money in our lives. We were not living in poverty but we had plenty of bills, mainly doctor bills. But we were happy. We could see that that was not always the case when people had lots of money. What if this new job should become a huge financial success? How would we react?

We finally made an agreement between ourselves and with God that if we ever received an abundant income we would not seek material excess. Instead we would use our resources to raise good children and to do God's will as we saw it. At that time we didn't foresee the ramifications of that pact, but it was the beginning of our responsiveness to opportunities that unfolded.

After starting the engineering job, Bob went back to school at San Jose State University. Sputnik was launched shortly after and the Russians flew their first intercontinental missile. The later-to-be-proved-false missile gap sparked national paranoia. Operational dates for the new Polaris submarines were moved ahead. Bob was working on the submarine-launched missiles and his engineering department went on a ten-hour-day, six-day-week schedule. In spite of this exhausting pace, Bob continued part time with college courses and, after five grueling years, managed to graduate with highest honors in his aeronautical engineering class.

Bob took a keen interest in his new engineering job and advanced rapidly. But other forces entered our lives shortly after we moved to Santa Clara. New acquaintances invited us to join the Christian Family Movement, a lay Christian movement that started in the United States and has now spread throughout the world to become a strong force for social change. It emphasizes the importance of the family. Meanwhile our own family continued to grow, until we had ten healthy children entrusted to our care. We were well blessed.

CFM had a strong formative effect on our spiritual life during the 11 years we were active, and in the years since. We worked with other couples in a close community spirit, sharing work projects and recreation. Eventually we saw beyond our own comfort and desired it for all people.

Another important jump in awareness came in 1963 when we made our Cursillo. The Cursillo (a little course in Christianity started in Spain) is an intense three-day experience in Christian love. It forced us to scrutinize ourselves and our commitment to God and humanity.

During his first eight years at Lockheed Bob helped design three generations of Polaris missiles. He worked mostly on wind tunnel testing and underwater launch development. During that time he was convinced that building weapons to deter war was his most important contribution to peace. Once a fellow worker engaged him in a philosophical discussion about religion in daily life and asked, "What do you think God wants you to do most of all?"

"Just what I am doing," Bob responded without hesitation. "To help design this missile to protect our country." Although the conversation died at that point, the question bothered him for time to come. But Bob had not yet learned to pay attention when disturbed.

In 1965 Lockheed cornered the Poseidon missile contract and Bob transferred to reentry systems. That is the part of the missile which carries the hydrogen bomb to its destination. He helped design the multiple individually targeted reentry vehicles (more commonly called MIRVs). MIRVs allow one missile to destroy many targets. Working on these, Bob saw what happens at the other end of the missile's flight.

It bothered him to hear how the Poseidon missile-submarine weapon was evaluated: that system has an "effectiveness" of killing one-quarter of Russia's population. Helping to prepare for such incineration was disquieting. Bob subconsciously resorted to moral self-deception: he dismissed that uncomfortable fact by simply not thinking about it. He did not visualize the killing, maiming, orphaning, and widowing that would take place if Poseidon were ever used, pursuing his work with the superficial awareness that one acquires through the daily newspaper.

Bob's real questioning of nuclear weapons started about 1968. After dinner one evening our oldest daughter, Janie, a sophomore at Santa Clara University at the time, was telling us about some campus demonstrations. Students were protesting against Dow Chemical because it made napalm to use in Vietnam. The discussion went into the wee hours of the morning. Janie expressed her concern that when the Vietnam issue was settled, the protest would turn to the building of nuclear weapons. Bob defended his position: these weapons were needed to prevent Russia from taking over the world. At the least, they were needed until a meaningful treaty could be negotiated. But Janie insisted that people must summon the courage to change their destructive behavior.

Bob was shaken. He had worked hard to complete college. His future was promising. We had a large family to support and it just wasn't realistic to think about starting over. But we were not reckoning on how God would present his desires and how we would respond. The obstacles seemed insurmountable at the time. They forced Bob to another form of self-deception: rationalizing. When troubling thoughts become too persistent to be repressed we often justify immoral activity with faulty logic.

A new consciousness did dawn on us, however. Bob became more aware of what was happening about him at work. He noticed that most of his fellow workers did not really seem convinced that they were defending their country. Patriotic feelings and good intentions took second place to winning contracts and keeping the business going. Lockheed puts much effort on future business—developing new weapons concepts with which to entice the military. The real motive behind the arms race gradually surfaced in our understanding: profits for the company and job security for the workers.

Bob describes how his work environment contributed to his growing uneasiness:

I observed very little joy within the guarded gates of Lockheed. Only the intellectual surfaced, and that was strictly along the lines of "me and my project." That sterile attitude, accompanied by tough competition to gain more responsibility, was the general rule. Why people wanted to gather more and more work under their control always amazed me. I finally diagnosed this "empire building" as groping for security—a need to become indispensable. But I knew of very few who achieved any degree of permanency. A budget cut or administrative reshuffle could result in being squeezed out of line in the pecking order.

I did not realize it at the time, but my interior attitude was shifting from a "thing-relationship" to concern for others—a change which tolled the death knell for my engineering career in the defense industry.

Bob became involved in subterfuge at Lockheed in 1970, involving the use of secret classifications to deceive the public. The first strategic arms limitation talks (SALT) were just getting under way. Simultaneously, a public outcry to ban the MIRV was gaining momentum. Lockheed and the Navy realized that such a ban could lead to cancellation of the Poseidon missile contract which would mean a profit loss for Lockheed, to say nothing of depriving the Navy of its newest weapon. A task force was set up to investigate other types of warheads which could be used on Poseidon in case MIRVs were outlawed.

At first this effort was openly called SALT Studies. But as the cry to ban the MIRV grew louder, it became apparent that this would be a sensitive issue if people found out that Lockheed and the Navy were trying to evade arms limitation. The task force was moved behind secret doors and given the code name of CAFE; the relationship between SALT negotiations and CAFE became secret information. It was clear that secrecy was being used only to prevent the American people from discerning the government's lack of sincerity in the area of disarmament.

It was about this time that design studies were started on the new Trident missile. Bob was then a leader of an advanced reentry system design group. He was given design responsibility for the maneuvering reentry vehicle (MARV) for Trident. To acquaint himself with maneuvering technology he reviewed many secret reports which revealed the Pentagon's interest in greater accuracy for missile warheads. Such precision was not needed according to our long-standing deterrent policy, which threatens massive retaliation only if attacked. Increased accuracy is only necessary if the Pentagon is planning to destroy targets, such as missile silos. To do that means shooting first; it doesn't make sense to retaliate against empty silos.

Bob saw this policy switch over three years before it was finally revealed to the American public. It had actually started about 1965 when the United States finished its buildup of intercontinental ballistic missiles and missile-launching submarines. Robert McNamara, Secretary of Defense at the time, said that U.S. emphasis would thereafter be on quality improvements. This led to a more aggressive military policy. Because of the overkill in deterrent capability, it was becoming harder to justify more weapons. But improving the quality still sounded reasonable—and that touched off a new sprint in the arms race.

We now read quite openly in the papers that the U.S. might use nuclear weapons first under some circumstances, but such brazen proclamations would not have been accepted at the beginning of this decade. In 1970 it had a traumatic effect on Bob to find them shrouded in secrecy.

No longer could he repress sinister facts from his thoughts, nor was rationalization effective. Another means was needed to salve his conscience. We became active as peace information coordinators for the National Association of Laity, a Catholic lay organization working for church renewal and social reform. In that work we were exposed to more international study and research.

The new knowledge of how multinational corporations' behavior, the substance of our own livelihood, was oppressing poor people at home and abroad made Bob's position even more untenable. We could see that our superficial involvement in peace work had no real roots. But we also tried to convince ourselves that if we were not enjoying the lush salary and ample fringe benefits from this macabre livelihood, they would only go to someone else. Yet I could see that Bob was being torn apart inside because of the work he was performing. I prepared myself psychologically for the impending change.

For slightly over a year we depended on bomb-building for our survival and worked for peace as a hobby. Eventually this hypocritical existence became unbearable. Early in 1972 we agreed that, regardless of the effect our action would have, we had to follow our consciences. We started planning our escape from the military-industrial complex. Bob would have to give up engineering, as it would be practically impossible to find such a job in our area not tied to a military contract.

It was important to us that the children should share in our decisions insofar as they were capable. We talked our plans over with them and answered their questions. At family meetings we let their fears and ours be heard.

We learned from the example of Jim and Shelley Douglass, whom we met in the first months of our "liberation plan." Jim's book, *Resistance and Contemplation: The Way of Liberation*, revealed their struggle to give up security and accept suffering for the whole family.

We had voiced the same fears and asked the same questions, but we hadn't listened well enough to understand the answers. We had to see someone actually try the road before we could venture on it. We had leaned too much on precedents, which were nothing more than crutches for our weak determination. Our subjective morality had to yield. We had to act on our own convictions.

We set the date for January of 1973. Immediately after the Christmas holidays Bob would tell Lockheed he was leaving. We would start the new year with a new life.

Having spent the past quarter-century caring for home and children, I started looking for a job immediately. I wanted to work with handicapped children and had been taking courses in vision therapy. But when I found an instructional aide opening in the school system, I took it. My job reflected our desire to deepen our marriage relationship by abolishing the traditional roles of husband and wife, and by sharing all the chores, joys, trials and responsibilities equally. The first overt step toward the transition was made.

During his last month on the job Bob discussed our decision with co-workers. Some were sympathetic and one even congratulated him for making the move. But they could not imagine taking similar action themselves. The need for financial security was too deeply ingrained. That singular fear is probably the greatest obstacle to moral action in today's society.

When the guarded gates of Lockheed clanged shut behind Bob for the last time, we started cutting expenses as an economical necessity. We ate less meat and experimented with new recipes that give a balanced diet at less expense. Second-hand shops became our source of clothing. We discovered ways to reduce spending and new approaches to pleasure without having to "buy" entertainment.

For us, simple living began by revising our work pattern. Work in the traditional sense usually occupied about half of our waking hours; we tended to center our lives around it, which prevented us from seeing our labor in proper context. It had become an end in itself, rather than the means of living; occupational success outshone all other values.

Living on a large salary, measuring success by income, does violence to the 94 percent of the world's population who must survive on only half the global wealth. We sometimes attempted to alleviate that disparity by donations to "charity," but that type of giving merely numbed our consciences, and in no way approached charity in its gospel sense. Ambrose, bishop of Milan during the fourth century, said about token giving: "You are not making a gift of your possessions to the poor man. You are handing over to him what is his. For what has been given in common for the use of all, you have arrogated to yourself."

There are arguments that one can live simply on a large salary while using the excess for good works, but we have never seen them lived out. Voluntary poverty is not a comfortable thought for the affluent and thus their judgment of simplicity becomes distorted. Too often worldly excesses are rationalized away by willingness to be "poor in spirit."

But a spirit of poverty amid wealth is impossible. That's why Jesus suggested selling all. Voluntary poverty does not mean destitution, but it does require putting our whole being into it. Our family has only scratched the surface of simple living. And the overall effort of trying to live a nonviolent life—wife, husband, and children together—is difficult, because affluence has become so deeply ingrained. But the main thing as we see it is that our family is feeling its way. To us that means really believing Jesus' teachings— saying we are Christians and trying to live it, saying we are nonviolent and trying to act nonviolently. We are trying to be less greedy as we search for ways to reduce our own needs so there will be enough to go around. Life is still scary, but we attempt to follow our consciences and rely on faith.

George Zabelka

A Military Chaplain

In August 1945, Fr. George Zabelka, a Catholic chaplain with the U.S. Army air force, was stationed on Tinian Island in the South Pacific. He served as priest and pastor for the airmen who dropped the atomic bombs on Hiroshima and Nagasaki.

He was discharged in 1946. During the next 20 years he gradually began to realize that what he had done and believed during the war was wrong, and that the only way he could be a Christian was to be a pacifist. He was deeply influenced in this process by the civil rights movement and the works of Martin Luther King, Jr. and Mahatma Gandhi.

In 1972 he met Charles C. McCarthy, a theologian, lawyer, and father of 10. McCarthy, who founded the Center for the Study of Nonviolence at the University of Notre Dame, was leading a workshop on nonviolence at Zabelka's church. The two men fell into the first of several conversations about the issues raised by the workshop. Some time later, Zabelka reached the conclusion that the use of violence under any circumstances was incompatible with his understanding of the gospel of Christ.

Now retired, Fr. Zabelka gives workshops on nonviolence and assists in diocesan work in Lansing, Michigan. The following is a recent interview with Zabelka, conducted by McCarthy.

Charles McCarthy: Father Zabelka, what is your relationship to the atomic bombing of Hiroshima and Nagasaki in August, 1945?
Fr. Zabelka: During the summer of 1945, July, August, and September, I was assigned as Catholic chaplain to the 509th Composite Group on Tinian Island. The 509th was the atomic bomb group.
McCarthy: What were your duties in relationship to these men?
Zabelka: The usual. I said mass on Sunday and during the week. Heard confessions. Talked with the boys, etc. Nothing significantly

14

different from what any other chaplain did during the war.

McCarthy: Did you know that the 509th was preparing to drop an atomic bomb?

Zabelka: No. We knew that they were preparing to drop a bomb substantially different from and more powerful than even the "blockbusters" used over Europe, but we never called it an atomic bomb and never really knew what it was before August 6, 1945. Before that time we just referred to it as the "gimmick" bomb.

McCarthy: So since you did not know that an atomic bomb was going to be dropped you had no reason to counsel the men in private or preach in public about the morality of such a bombing?

Zabelka: Well, that is true enough; I never did speak against it, nor could I have spoken against it since I, like practically everyone else on Tinian, was ignorant of what was being prepared. And I guess I will go to my God with that as my defense. But on Judgment Day I think I am going to need to seek more mercy than justice in this matter.

McCarthy: Why? God certainly could not have expected you to act on ideas that had never entered your mind.

Zabelka: As a Catholic priest my task was to keep my people, wherever they were, close to the mind and heart of Christ. As a military chaplain I was to try to see that the boys conducted themselves according to the teachings of the Catholic Church and Christ on war. When I look back I am not sure I did either of these things very well.

McCarthy: Why do you think that?

Zabelka: What I do not mean to say is that I feel myself to have been remiss in any duties that were expected of me as a chaplain. I saw that the mass and the sacraments were available as best I could. I even went out and earned paratroop wings in order to do my job better. Nor did I fail to teach and preach what the Church expected me to teach and preach—and I don't mean by this that I just talked to the boys about their sexual lives. I and most chaplains were quite clear and outspoken on such matters as not killing and torturing prisoners. But there were other areas where things were not said quite so clearly.

McCarthy: For example?

Zabelka: The destruction of civilians in war was always forbidden by the Church, and if a soldier came to me and asked if he could put a bullet through a child's head, I would have told him absolutely not. That would be mortally sinful. But in 1945 Tinian Island was the largest airfield in the world. Three planes a minute could take off from it around the clock. Many of these planes went to Japan with the express purpose of killing not one child or one civilian but of slaughtering hundreds and thousands and tens of thousands of children and civilians—and I said nothing.

McCarthy: Why not? You certainly knew civilians were being destroyed by the thousands in these raids, didn't you?

Zabelka: Oh, indeed I did know, and I knew with a clarity that few others could have had.

McCarthy: What do you mean?

Zabelka: As a chaplain I often had to enter the world of the boys who were losing their minds because of something they did in war. I remember one young man who was engaged in the bombings of the cities of Japan. He was in the hospital on Tinian Island on the verge of a complete mental collapse.

He told me that he had been on a low-level bombing mission, flying right down one of the main streets of the city, when straight ahead of him appeared a little boy, in the middle of the street, looking up at the plane in childlike wonder. The man knew that in a few seconds this child would be burned to death by napalm which had already been released.

Yes, I knew civilians were being destroyed and knew it perhaps in a way others didn't. Yet I never preached a single sermon against killing civilians to the men who were doing it.

McCarthy: Again, why not?

Zabelka: Because I was "brainwashed"! It never entered my mind to publicly protest the consequences of these massive air raids. I was told it was necessary; told openly by the military and told implicitly by my Church's leadership. To the best of my knowledge no American cardinals or bishops were opposing these mass air raids. Silence in such matters, especially by a public body like the American bishops, is a stamp of approval.

The whole structure of the secular, religious, and military society told me clearly that it was all right to "let the Japs have it." God was on the side of my country. The Japanese were the enemy, and I was absolutely certain of my country's and Church's teaching about enemies; no erudite theological text was necessary to tell me. The day-in-day-out operation of the state and the Church between 1940 and 1945 spoke more clearly about Christian attitudes toward enemies and war than St. Augustine or St. Thomas Aquinas ever could.

I was certain that this mass destruction was right, certain to the point that the question of its morality never seriously entered my mind. I was "brainwashed" not by force or torture but by my Church's silence and whole-hearted cooperation in thousands of little ways with the country's war machine. Why, after I finished chaplaincy school at Harvard I had my military chalice officially blessed by the then Bishop Cushing of Boston. How much more clearly could the message be given? Indeed, I was "brainwashed"!

McCarthy: So you feel that because you did not protest the morality of the bombing of other cities with their civilian populations, that somehow you are morally responsible for the dropping of the atomic bomb?

Zabelka: The facts are that seventy-five thousand people were burned to death in one evening of fire bombing over Tokyo. Hundreds of thousands were destroyed in Dresden, Hamburg, and Coventry by aerial bombing. The fact that forty-five thousand human beings were killed by one bomb over Nagasaki was new only to the extent that it was one bomb that did it.

To fail to speak to the utter moral corruption of the mass destruction of civilians was to fail as a Christian and a priest as I see it. Hiroshima and Nagasaki happened in and to a world and a Christian church that had asked for it—that had prepared the moral consciousness of humanity to do and to justify the unthinkable. I am sure there are church documents around someplace bemoaning civilian deaths in modern war, and I am sure those in power in the church will drag them out to show that it was giving moral leadership during World War II to its membership.

Well, I was there, and I'll tell you that the operational moral atmosphere in the church in relation to mass bombing of enemy civilians was totally indifferent, silent, and corrupt at best—at worst it was religiously supportive of these activities by blessing those who did them.

I say all this not to pass judgment on others, for I do not know their souls then or now. I say all this as one who was part of the so-called Christian leadership of the time. So you see, that is why I am not going to the day of judgment looking for justice in this matter. Mercy is my salvation.

McCarthy: You said the atomic bombing of Nagasaki happened to a church that "had asked for it." What do you mean by that?

Zabelka: For the first three centuries, the three centuries closest to Christ, the church was a pacifist church. With Constantine the church accepted the pagan Roman ethic of a just war and slowly began to involve its membership in mass slaughter, first for the state and later for the faith.

Catholics, Orthodox, and Protestants, whatever other differences they may have had on theological esoterica, all agreed that Jesus' clear and unambiguous teaching on the rejection of violence and on love of enemies was not to be taken seriously. And so each of the major branches of Christianity by different theological methods modified our Lord's teaching in these matters until all three were able to do what Jesus rejected, that is, take an eye for an eye, slaughter, maim, torture.

It seems a "sign" to me that seventeen hundred years of Christian terror and slaughter should arrive at August 6, 1945, when Catholics dropped the A-bomb on top of the largest and first Catholic city in Japan. One would have thought that I, as a Catholic priest, would have spoken out against the atomic bombing of nuns. (Three orders of Catholic sisters were destroyed in Nagasaki that day.) One would have thought that I would have suggested that as a minimal standard of Catholic morality, Catholics shouldn't bomb Catholic children. I didn't.

I, like the Catholic pilot of the Nagasaki plane, "The Great Artiste," was heir to a Christianity that had for seventeen hundred years engaged in revenge, murder, torture, the pursuit of power, and prerogative violence, all in the name of our Lord.

I walked through the ruins of Nagasaki right after the war and visited the place where once stood the Urakami Cathedral. I picked up a piece of a censer from the rubble. When I look at it today I pray God forgives us for how we have distorted Christ's teaching and destroyed his world by the distortion of that teaching. I was the Catholic chaplain who was there when this grotesque process that began with Constantine reached its lowest point—so far.

McCarthy: What do you mean by "so far"?

Zabelka: Briefly, what I mean is that I do not see that the moral climate in relation to war inside or outside the church has dramatically changed much since 1945. The mainline Christian churches still teach something that Christ never taught or even hinted at, namely the just war theory, a theory that to me has been completely discredited theologically, historically, and psychologically.

So as I see it, until the various churches within Christianity repent and begin to proclaim by word and deed what Jesus proclaimed in relation to violence and enemies, there is no hope for anything other than ever-escalating violence and destruction.

Until membership in the church means that a Christian chooses not to engage in violence for any reason and instead chooses to love, pray for, help, and forgive all enemies; until membership in the church means that Christians may not be members of any military—American, Polish, Russian, English, Irish, et al.; until membership in the church means that the Christian cannot pay taxes for others to kill others; and until the church says these things in a fashion which the simplest soul could understand—until that time humanity can only look forward to more dark nights of slaughter on a scale unknown in history. Unless the church unswervingly and unambiguously teaches what Jesus teaches on this matter it will not be the divine leaven in the human dough that it was meant to be.

"The choice is between nonviolence or nonexistence," as Martin Luther King, Jr., said, and he was not, and I am not, speaking figuratively. It is about time for the church and its leadership in all denominations to get down on its knees and repent of this misrepresentation of Christ's words.

Communion with Christ cannot be established on disobedience to his clearest teachings. Jesus authorized none of his followers to substitute violence for love; not me, not you, not Ronald Reagan, not the pope, not a Vatican council, nor even an ecumenical council.

McCarthy: Father Zabelka, what kinds of immediate steps do you think the church should take in order to become the "divine leaven in the human dough"?

Zabelka: Step one should be that Christians the world over should be taught that Christ's teaching to love their enemies is not optional. I've been in many parishes in my life, and I have found none where the congregation explicitly is called upon regularly to pray for its enemies. I think this is essential.

I offer you step two at the risk of being considered hopelessly out of touch with reality. I would like to suggest that there is an immediate need to call an ecumenical council for the specific purpose of clearly declaring that war is totally incompatible with Jesus' teaching and that Christians cannot and will not engage in or pay for it from this point in history on. This would have the effect of putting all nations on this planet on notice that from now on they are going to have to conduct their mutual slaughter without Christian support—physical, financial, or spiritual.

I am sure there are other issues which Catholics or Orthodox or Protestants would like to confront in an ecumenical council instead of the facing up to the hard teachings of Christ in relationship to violence and enemies. But it seems to me that issues like the meaning of the primacy of Peter are nowhere near as pressing or as destructive of church credibility and God's world as is the problem of continued Christian participation in and justification of violence and slaughter. I think the church's continued failure to speak clearly Jesus' teachings is daily undermining its credibility and authority in all other areas.

McCarthy: Do you think there is the slightest chance that the various branches of Christianity would come together in an ecumenical council for the purpose of declaring war and violence totally unacceptable activities for Christians under all circumstances?

Zabelka: Remember, I prefaced my suggestion of an ecumenical council by saying that I risked being considered hopelessly out of touch with reality. On the other hand, what is impossible for men and women is quite possible for God if people will only use their freedom to cooperate a little.

Who knows what could happen if the pope, the patriarch of Constantinople, and the president of the World Council of Churches called with one voice for such a council? One thing I am sure of is that our Lord would be very happy if his church were again unequivocally teaching what he unequivocally taught on the subject of violence.

Billy Graham

An Evangelist

*In recent years many fresh voices in the church have been
speaking out with a Christian witness against the insanity of the
nuclear arms race. One of the most surprising and significant of
these is Billy Graham's. He believes that the nation and the world
now face their own hour of decision about halting the escalation of
nuclear weapons. Graham's growing convictions, which he describes as a change from past years, have taken firm root and are
now becoming one of his most deeply felt concerns as a Christian.
In 1979 Graham agreed to share his thinking publicly by responding to these questions posed by Wes Michaelson and Jim Wallis,
from* Sojourners *magazine.*

Sojourners: When you were in Poland at Auschwitz last year, you
said, "The present insanity of the global arms race, if continued,
will lead inevitably to a conflagration so great that Auschwitz will
seem like a minor rehearsal." Would you share further your feelings about the nuclear arms race?

Billy Graham: The present arms race is a terrifying thing, and it is
almost impossible to overestimate its potential for disaster. There is
something ironic about the fact that we live in a generation which
has made unprecedented advances in such fields as public health
and medicine, and yet never before has the threat of wholesale destruction been so real—all because of human technology.

Is a nuclear holocaust inevitable if the arms race is not
stopped? Frankly, the answer is almost certainly yes. Now I know
that some people feel human beings are so terrified of a nuclear
war that no one would dare start one. I wish I could accept that.
But neither history nor the Bible gives much reason for optimism.
What guarantee is there that the world will never produce another
maniacal dictator like Hitler or Amin?

As a Christian I take sin seriously, and the Christian should be the first to know that the human heart is deceitful and desperately wicked, as Jeremiah says. We can be capable of unspeakable horror, no matter how educated or technically sophisticated we are. Auschwitz is a compelling witness to this.

I know not everyone would agree with this, but I honestly wish we had never developed nuclear weapons. But of course that is water under the bridge. We have nuclear weapons in horrifying quantities, and the question is, what are we going to do about it?

Sojourners: How does your commitment to the lordship of Christ shape your response to the nuclear threat?

Graham: I am not sure I have thought through all the implications of Christ's lordship for this issue—I have to be honest about that. But for the Christian there is—or at least should be—only one question: What is the will of God? What is his will both for this world and for me in regard to this issue?

Let me suggest several things. First, the lordship of Christ reminds me that we live in a sinful world. The cross teaches me that. Like a drop of ink in a glass of water, sin has permeated everything—the individual, society, creation. That is one reason why the nuclear issue is not just a political issue—it is a moral and spiritual issue as well. And because we live in a sinful world it means we have to take something like nuclear armaments seriously. We know the terrible violence of which the human heart is capable.

Secondly, the lordship of Jesus Christ tells me that God is not interested in destruction, but in redemption. Christ came to seek and to save that which was lost. He came to reverse the effects of the Fall.

Now I know there are mysteries to the workings of God. I know God is sovereign and sometimes he permits things to happen which are evil, and he even causes the wrath of man to praise him. But I cannot see any way in which nuclear war could be branded as being God's will. Such warfare, if it ever happens, will come because of the greed and pride and covetousness of the human heart. But God's will is to establish his kingdom, in which Christ is lord.

Third, of course, Christ calls us to love, and that is the critical test of discipleship. Love is not a vague feeling or an abstract idea. When I love someone, I seek what is best for them. If I begin to take the love of Christ seriously, then I will work toward what is best for my neighbor. I will seek to bind up the wounds and bring

22

about healing, no matter what the cost may be.

Therefore, I believe that the Christian especially has a responsibility to work for peace in our world. Christians may well find themselves working and agreeing with non-believers on an issue like peace. But our motives will not be identical.

The issues are not simple, and we are always tempted to grasp any program which promises easy answers. Or, on the other side, we are tempted to say that the issues are too complex, and we cannot do anything of significance anyway. We must resist both temptations.

Sojourners: How would you describe the changes in your thinking on the nuclear arms question, and what factors would you cite as important in prompting those changes?

Graham: It has only been relatively recently (sort of a pilgrimage over the last few years) that I have given as much attention to this subject as it deserves. I suppose there have been a number of reasons why I have come to be concerned about it. For one thing, during my travels in recent years I have spoken to a number of leaders in many countries. Almost to a person they have been concerned and pessimistic about the nuclear arms race.

Second, I think also that I have been helped by other Christians who have been sensitive to this issue. I guess I would have to admit that the older I get the more aware I am of the kind of world my generation has helped shape, and the more concerned I am about doing what I can to give the next generation at least some hope for peace. I have fourteen grandchildren now, and I ask myself, "What kind of world are they going to face?"

Third, I have gone back to the Bible to restudy what it says about the responsibilities we have as peacemakers. I have seen that we must seek the good of the whole human race, and not just the good of any one nation or race.

There have been times in the past when I have, I suppose, confused the kingdom of God with the American way of life. Now I am grateful for the heritage of our country, and I am thankful for many of its institutions and ideals, in spite of its many faults. But the kingdom of God is not the same as America, and our nation is subject to the judgment of God just as much as any other nation.

I have become concerned to build bridges of understanding among nations and want to do whatever I can to help this. We live in a different world than we did a hundred years ago, or even a generation ago. We cannot afford to neglect our duties as global citizens. Like it or not, the world is a very small place, and what one nation does affects all others. That is especially true concerning nuclear weapons.

Sojourners: Have your crusades and experiences in Eastern Europe influenced your thinking on the arms race? Do you feel that the differences between the East and the West are worth nuclear war?

Graham: The opportunities I have had to visit Yugoslavia, Hungary, and Poland have been very significant. I went with many stereotypes in my mind, but I came away with a new understanding especially of how the church exists and in some instances thrives in these societies—and a new awareness of their concerns about peace.

I especially was impressed with the concerns various Christians in these countries expressed about peace. I believe their concern is genuine, and they have something to teach us here. Take Poland, for instance. They have a long history of invasion and occupation, climaxing in the horror of Nazi occupation and terror. They know that a war would bring them to the brink of destruction, especially in the nuclear age.

I think Americans sometimes forget how fortunate we have been, because we have not known what it is to have a war on our own territory since the Civil War. It has tended to make us complacent, I think, and has made us forget the destruction and disruption war brings.

To answer the rest of your question: No. I do not think the present differences are worth a nuclear war. There is no denying that there are differences between us. But there are many things we have in common, especially on an ordinary human level. I am not a pacifist, but I fervently hope and pray our differences will never become an excuse for nuclear war. I hold the view that some wars had to be fought in history, such as the war against the Nazis. The alternative would have been worse.

Sojourners: A year ago several evangelical leaders joined with others in signing "A Call to Faithfulness," a declaration committing themselves as Christians against nuclear weapons. The Southern Baptists recently held a convocation on the nuclear crisis, and others, including the National Association of Evangelicals, have begun making statements opposing the arms race. What has been your response to such developments, and what significance do you see in them?

Graham: These are highly significant, because they indicate a new awareness (especially on the part of evangelicals) of the arms race and the responsibilities we have to work for peace. I have encouraged such statements, but more than that I am encouraging evangelicals not just to make statements but to go beyond them and get involved in various ways.

There was a time when evangelicals were in the vanguard of some of the great social movements. I think of the fight against the slave trade, for example. Then in some respects we lost sight of our responsibilities to fight social evils. We said that the world would never be reformed completely anyway until Christ came again, so why bother? But of course that was evading the issue. After all, I know that not everyone will believe the gospel, but that does not mean I should give up preaching it. I know the human race is not going to suddenly be converted to Christ but that does not keep me from preaching him. I also know the nations are not going to suddenly lay down their arms but that does not keep us from doing all we can before it is too late.

Now I think evangelicals are regaining their social concern, seeing that God is concerned about the whole person. There is a danger that we will go to the opposite extreme and reduce the gospel to social activism, of course. But what we all need to do is return to the Bible afresh—not going to it to prove a point, but seeing what it says as the Holy Spirit opens our eyes. We need to see what it says about our priorities, our lifestyles, and our mission in the world. Then we need to obey. I think evangelicals are seeing this, and the things you mention are evidence.

Sojourners: What word would you have for the church, and specifically the evangelical community, on this issue?

Graham: First, we cannot wash our hands of our responsibilities. What some people do not see is that failing to oppose something may at times actually be condoning it. God is concerned about every area of life, and Christ's lordship means we also must be concerned about every area of our lives and seek to bring everything under that lordship.

Second, we must place the will of God before all else. Is it his will that resources be used for massive armaments which could otherwise be used for alleviating human suffering and hunger? Of course not. Our world has lost sight of true values and substituted false gods and false values.

Finally, we must do what we can, both individually and collectively, to try to bring some sanity into our world.

Sojourners: What should Christians in the United States be saying and doing to reverse government policies that are escalating the nuclear arms race?

Graham: This is a very complex issue, and I believe it demands the energy and thoughtfulness of the whole Christian community. I would not pretend to have a complete answer by any means.

However, the first thing we must do is understand the issues. I think many Christians are only just beginning to see that the nuclear arms race is an entirely new factor in human history, and that we cannot be complacent about it or treat it as just another minor issue. We need to educate the Christian community about the moral and ethical issues which are involved.

Then we must do what we can to work for policy change where it is needed. I do not favor unilateral disarmament, but we must sometimes be willing to take risks (within limits) as a nation. It is here that we need to think carefully about what we are doing.

Within our system it is possible to bring about changes, and we need to let our voices be heard by those we have elected. I would also say this to Christians of other nations that have or are developing nuclear weapons.

But let's remember also that the most important thing we can do is to pray. I believe we ought to be praying for the leaders of our world—not just our president, but the leaders of every major country. And we ought to pray for Christians in other countries, especially ones which are very different from our own nation, that God would give them wisdom and courage to work for peace. Sometimes we forget that prayer is our most powerful weapon, even if we may not understand how God can use our prayers.

Sojourners: How do such responses to the arms race affect the credibility of the evangelical witness throughout the world?

Graham: Well, of course we should take a stand for what is right, whether it helps our visibility in the world or not.

But I believe this is a very crucial issue for the whole world, and because of it, the world is going to be watching us very closely. Our works must always back up our words, and it is certainly true on this issue.

Sojourners: As you know, Senator Mark O. Hatfield has indicated his possible opposition to the SALT II treaty because it will permit the U.S. to build a new generation of nuclear weapons systems—such as the cruise missile, Trident, and the MX missile. What is your reaction, and your feelings regarding the SALT II treaty?

Graham: A treaty such as this is highly technical, of course. As I understand it, it is not a comprehensive treaty; there are vast areas which are untouched, and this concerns me. Some of the worst and most sophisticated weapons are not involved. Furthermore, nothing is done about some of the frightful weapons which are even now being developed—weapons which would be far more advanced technically than present weapon systems. These weapons which are waiting in the wings concern me greatly.

Personally, however, I think a major factor must be another question. What will happen if the treaty is not passed? Granted, the treaty will not bring the arms race to a halt. Some say it will escalate it. But if the treaty is not approved, I fear not only escalation but the psychological effects on the world.

If SALT II were the final treaty we would ever negotiate for arms limitation, then relatively little has been accomplished. But these things have to be taken one step at a time. SALT II should give way to SALT III. I wish we were working on SALT X right now! Total destruction of nuclear arms.

We have taken years to make even the limited progress we have achieved in the U.S.-Soviet relations. We must do whatever we can to make this fragile relationship more secure. We have to take a long-range view, and not seek some temporary short-term advantage or solution which will only harm the chances for reconciliation with the Soviet Union. This is true whether we are speaking about nuclear arms limitation or our relationship with China, or any other foreign policy issue.

We may be living on the edge of Armageddon. I do not know; this may be one of God's great springtimes in human history. Jesus told us to watch the signs of the times. The signs I see are both ominous and hopeful.

I know one thing—the ultimate hope of the world is the coming of the Prince of Peace—when war shall be no more. Even so, come, Lord Jesus.

Thomas Gumbleton, Raymond Hunthausen, Leroy Matthiesen, and Walter Sullivan

Four Bishops

In November of 1981 the bishops of the U.S. Catholic Church held their annual meeting in Washington, D.C. In his opening address, Archbishop John Roach, president of the National Conference of Catholic Bishops, called the bishops to leadership in efforts to stop the arms race, ban abortion, and advocate for the poor.

"On a global scale, the most dangerous moral issue in the public order today is the nuclear arms race. . . . The church needs to say 'no' clearly and decisively to the use of nuclear arms," he said.

Later Archbishop Joseph Bernadin, chairman of the Bishops' Committee on War and Peace, gave a report on the group's work that carefully reiterated the church's historical teachings on war and its growing concern over nuclear war.

Among the 270 prelates making up the conference were Bishops Thomas Gumbleton of Detroit, Raymond Hunthausen of Seattle, Leroy Matthiesen of Amarillo, Texas, and Walter Sullivan of Richmond, Virginia. Each has made statements and taken actions that place them clearly against the nation's policies concerning nuclear weapons.

In June 1981, Hunthausen asked the Catholics of Seattle to think about refusing to pay half their income tax in protest of the amount of revenue spent on nuclear arms. Later that summer Matthiesen asked workers at an Amarillo nuclear munitions plant to consider finding other work.

While in town for the conference, these four bishops spent an evening talking to a crowded assembly hall at Catholic University where they responded to questions about their positions, faith journeys, and hopes for the church. Later that night, three of them were interviewed for Sojourners *by Jim Wallis. Following is an edited transcript of their statements and the subsequent interview.*

Bishop Thomas Gumbleton: My position is simple to state: I am a total pacifist. I would not accept the use of any form of violence in my own defense. Of course we can never say for sure how we would act in all circumstances, but I would always try to reject violence. I feel that the Christian faith and the gospel message compel me to reject war—nuclear and conventional war.

Now, I know that sounds very simple, decisive, and definitive; and yet I have to say that I am amazed at myself because that's not where I started. I grew up in a typical Catholic family. I was too young to participate in World War II (I was in elementary school), but I can remember three of my brothers going into the service. I remember how hard it was for our family, but no one ever thought for a moment that there was any other option. A good Catholic made his contribution for his country and went to war. There was no question about it.

I later went to seminary, took all the usual courses in theology, and studied the just war theology briefly. I accepted it completely and preached it as a Catholic priest; when I was ordained I never had second thoughts about it.

In the '60s I was assigned to work in the chancellery of my diocese at the time that priests and sisters shocked a lot of people by being on the picket lines and in demonstrations against the Vietnam War. We had priests in our diocese who were opposed to the war and were going public, and it was getting to be a little embarrassing. Since I was the youngest priest at the chancellery, the bishop suggested that I could talk to them and ask them to back off a little.

So I tried; I went and visited these priests, and we got into some good discussions. Before I knew it, I began to understand what they were doing and why, and I began to change my thinking. Within another year or two I was on some of those marches and in demonstrations, and I was forced to think and pray.

An author who had influenced my life a lot in seminary was Thomas Merton. I looked at what he wrote about nonviolence. I had never really noticed it before. I searched Dorothy Day's works more carefully, and also the writings of someone who was a sort of hero of mine, Gordon Zahn.

Surprisingly, in 1968 I was ordained a bishop. I got involved in the Bishops' Conference and pushed for statements such as the resolution of 1971 against the Vietnam War. Since I was forced into a more public position, I had to think things through even more carefully. Not only did I go back to some of the writers I had come to appreciate more, but I made a very careful attempt to search out the Scriptures. I came to a deep and firmly held conclusion that, in the words of the scholar John MacKenzie, Jesus taught us not how to kill but how to die, and he rejected violence for any reason.

I did not come to this conclusion quickly or easily. When I first took a stand against the war, I hadn't even thought about violence and nonviolence; I was against the Vietnam War on the basis of just war theology.

There is absolutely no question that the violence of nuclear war is beyond any rational understanding of even a just war theology. And so my position in regard to the nuclear arms race and the policy of the United States is consistent with my strong conviction about nonviolence.

But I would insist that anyone who is going to follow the nonviolent words of Christ will have to go through a spiritual conversion. It won't happen through logical argumentation. I thank God that to some extent at least that conversion has happened within myself. And I continue to pray daily that I will deepen in this conversion, because I am convinced that it is the way that Jesus leads us.

Bishop Raymond Hunthausen: I heard Bishop Gumbleton say that he is a total pacifist. I've never said that about myself. I've always said that I am a nuclear pacifist; but given our present world, it is unrealistic to talk about conventional war. So maybe it's time for me to say that I am a total pacifist, in our current global context.

I was in college when World War II erupted, and I saw many of my closest friends go into the military. I struggled to decide whether to go to seminary or into the military. I was involved in a civilian pilot training program, and I was excited about the prospect of moving into what the government called the secondary program. I wanted to do aerobatics, but it was clear that if one was in the program and the United States entered the war, one would automatically be in the Air Force.

My spiritual director helped me to see that I had to give my call and vocation to the priesthood a chance, so I opted for the seminary; but I would have to say that at the time I certainly felt keenly about going into the military.

I was in the seminary in 1945 when the atomic bombs hit Hiroshima and Nagasaki. I'll never forget that day, because I was appalled; I just could not believe what had happened, that there was an instrument of destruction as awesome as this bomb. I was caught up in a great turmoil wondering, worrying, praying about this, and I could not grasp that our world had totally changed.

Well, I was ordained and lived with this reality just like the rest of the world, and though I wondered about much of the upheaval in our world, I didn't do anything about it.

I was appointed bishop in 1962. Another bishop was working with the synod on a statement about the ICBMs being deployed in Montana. We made a number of such statements, the first public witnesses that I, with others, was willing to take. It frightened me to death. I wasn't sure of my position, and I had that sense of being unpatriotic. I also got involved in a counseling service for conscientious objectors.

I went to Seattle in 1975 and wasn't there very long when I was visited by a most interesting and wonderful person, Jim Douglass of the Pacific Life Community. A pacifist, he has written a number of books, taught in universities, and given himself completely to the cause of peace. As he talked I realized that what he was saying coincided with how I felt; but I wasn't doing anything about it.

On his third visit he said he was going to Washington, D.C., to be with a group of people who were fasting in prayerful resistance to the position the U.S. had assumed in being willing to take first-strike initiatives. I felt compelled to write to the priests of the diocese to cite that fact and to quote from something I had read by Father Dick McSorley, who had written in the *U.S. Catholic* that the taproot of violence in our society is our willingness to live with nuclear destruction. I wrote to the priests that we had to be much more serious about this in our own lives, our preaching, and our praying.

After that I was more willing to say something publicly on my stance, and I was invited into some of our parishes, particularly those in the military areas. I said yes to one parish council and discovered when I arrived that the hall was filled. That was a very interesting and important moment in my life, because I was able to

31

discover the various positions and responses of people, and it helped me to understand the impact this was having on the people I was trying to serve.

I was invited by a Lutheran bishop to speak at a synod in Tacoma, Washington, in June of last year. I had a speech prepared that said something about the need to consider unilateral disarmament. A day or so before the speech, I decided to include something about taxes, because I had met a young man for whom I had great respect who was working for the Seattle Church Council, and I learned from him that he had been withholding war taxes for some time. He was very conscientious about it, very prayerful and serious.

Many people wonder how they might address the issue of nuclear weapons. Certainly we can pray and write to our Congresspeople, but sometimes people need to think about the implications in their own lives. So I spoke about withholding war taxes as a feasible strategy. I thought maybe my remarks would create a stir, rattle around Seattle for a couple of days, and go away. But they didn't. They stayed around. I must say it bothered me that the media picked up on the issue of taxes and lost the crux of what I really wanted to say, which was that the issue of nuclear weapons is one that prompts us to be men and women of faith and ask if we have put our security in our weaponry rather than in God.

Bishop Leroy Matthiesen: I count myself a real Johnny-come-lately to the issue Bishops Gumbleton, Hunthausen, and Sullivan have been involved in; but I really shudder to see the specter of monstrous mushroom clouds over Pantex, the plant where all the nuclear warheads manufactured in the United States are assembled. I live 15 miles from it, and for 10 years previously I lived four miles away and never said a word about it—until August of this year. I have been thrust into the issue very rapidly, and my head is still dizzy.

I can't explain why I wasn't involved earlier. I guess I knew about Pantex. I knew about it during World War II when it manufactured conventional bombs and bullets. There's a nice sign near it on Highway 50 that says "Department of Energy Research and Development Division." You can drive by there without any idea of what's going on. I must confess that I suspected but never dared to ask.

I got into the issue very quickly when a permanent deacon of our diocese came to me with his wife and asked for spiritual advice. They had gone through the diaconate program and had studied the theological issues of justice and peace. They had both come to the conclusion that what he was doing at the plant was immoral, and they wanted to know what I thought.

Well, that sent me looking; I went back to the sources, and I was shocked to find that Pius XII had had something to say about the issue in 1942; Pope Paul VI, John XXIII, and John Paul II all spoke of it too—every one of them unequivocally condemned the production, deployment, possession, use, and the threat to use nuclear weapons.

Let me illustrate the moral problem. On October 31, 1981, the day before All Saints, there was a brutal murder next door to me. At four o'clock in the morning, a young man broke into our convent and raped and murdered a 76-year-old sister. The town was in shock, particularly the Catholic community, and we had a very emotional and soul-searching funeral service.

About the same time I read a story about Father George Zabelka, who was the chaplain of the men who flew the bombers over Japan during World War II. Father Zabelka has become a committed peacemaker. The pilot of the bomber that delivered the bomb over Nagasaki was Catholic, and Father Zabelka tells how that pilot and others came to him with problems of conscience. Father Zabelka said he knew that we Americans were killing civilians, but he never preached a single sermon against it.

The point of my story is that on October 31, 1981, one man killed one Catholic sister, and we were in an uproar in Amarillo. On August 9, 1945, a Catholic chaplain told a Catholic pilot and the other men that what they were doing was necessary; and what they did on that day was to wipe out three entire orders of Catholic sisters in 30 minutes.

What is the difference? Some say that the difference is that we saved many American lives by ending the war quickly—from which I conclude that American lives must be more precious in the eyes of God than Japanese lives. For me that settles the moral question about the use of atomic bombs.

Last summer I heard the announcement about the assembling of the neutron bomb. I thought it strange that nobody made a statement against a bomb that opened the illusion that we could have a limited nuclear war. So I made my statement and set out the moral

33

issue as I saw it. Nuclear weapons throw out any concept of just warfare. They are immoral; and if that's true, then it's immoral for us to build, assemble, deploy, and threaten to use them. I called on the workers that were involved in building them to reflect on what they were doing, to consider the possibility of resigning and of going into other work.

Bishop Walter Sullivan: I come from Virginia, which has more military personnel than any other state in the union. The number-one industry in Virginia is the military. I take pride in saying publicly that I am not a pacifist. I got involved in the issue of nuclear weapons by accident. I was down at Virginia Beach sunning myself in 1971. I was preparing to talk to the Knights of Columbus, and during my stay at the beach I thought to myself, "I'll give a talk on peace." I started off by saying that Jesus is our peace and we are involved in a war that is tearing our country apart, and we ought to be concerned about it. It was a lousy talk, by the way; but by the middle of it I realized that I was giving everybody indigestion. The hostility got stronger, so I got stronger. By the end I thought the Knights of Columbus were going to draw their swords and come at me.

After 45 minutes of people yelling at me, a marine sergeant came up to me. He was the only person in that audience of 500 who said, "I want to thank you." I had spoken about conscientious objectors, and the sergeant continued, "Tonight you've saved for me my son. My son wants to be a conscientious objector, and I was faced with a decision about that. Now I know what I have to do."

That started me on the journey. I had for about 10 years been encouraging the peace movement but had never really entered it that deeply.

Last August I was back in Virginia Beach giving a talk on peace. The next day's newspaper headline was, "Bishop says nuclear arms are immoral." There's no question in my mind that we are dealing with idolatry of the worst kind by putting our security in nuclear armaments.

The church's teaching on nuclear weapons is the best-kept secret in the world. People didn't know where I was coming from when I spoke on war and peace. We have to link our faith with the question of peacemaking. Once you go to the roots of Scripture and to the person of Jesus, you can no longer tolerate nuclear armaments and the possibility of total destruction. There's no compromise.

Matthiesen: A growing number of bishops are becoming involved in the issue of nuclear weapons. They are examining their positions, and many are taking a position similar to the one taken by us here tonight. When I joined Pax Christi [the Catholic peace organization] in the spring, there were 16 bishops listed as members. I understand that before this conference began there were 52. Twenty bishops have made public statements calling for an end to the arms race.

Someone reported to me that Arthur Jones from the *National Catholic Reporter* was covering today's meeting, and his assessment of what went on this afternoon after hearing Archbishop Bernadin's progress report on a pastoral letter that will come out in November, 1982, on war and peace is that the ballgame is over as far as the church and the United States is concerned. In other words, the Catholic church in the United States will be a peace church.

Hunthausen: It was a very exciting afternoon. I felt tremendous support from most of the bishops. But we will be a peace church only if we as individuals are able to come to grips with what nonviolence really means in our own lives. It is not good enough to simply say what peace means. It demands a great deal of inward looking, of prayer, of letting go and acknowledging in faith that Jesus is Lord.

That faith begins with each of us individually, and it has to consume the church. Otherwise we are not going to be peacemakers, and we will not truly represent Jesus who is the Prince of Peace. I feel that our faith has to underlie everything we say on the subject no matter where or when we say it.

Gumbleton: The overall impression of the afternoon was that there was a very strong commitment that the bishops of this country are going to give leadership in this area of war and peace. And we're going to try to make the Catholic teaching as plain as it can be and commit ourselves to encourage that teaching in every church in this country. In every way that we can, we will be active in trying to influence the public policy of the United States in accord with the teachings as we put them together in the document that will come out a year from now.

I was much impressed with the report in the beginning when Archbishop Bernadin insisted that we have to build on the Vatican Council II document on the pastoral constitution of the church in the modern world. In that document the bishops of the council called for a whole new attitude toward war.

This is going to require a profound conversion. We will not be a peace church because we have statements. We will only be a peace church when every one of us has profoundly changed our attitude toward war, and that can only happen through prayer and deep personal conversion.

So I would make the plea, like Archbishop Hunthausen, that each one of us commit ourselves to the journey of conversion. Those of us in the military, those working in the arms industry, those of us who pay taxes that support these activities must look at our lives thoroughly and ask ourselves whether we are engaged in this conversion, which is not intellectual but spiritual. Only then will we have a new attitude toward war that will allow us to respond to what John Paul II has said in his peace statements. He says, "I invite all Christians to bring to the task of building peace the specific contribution of the gospel." And, "In light of that gospel, I plead that you reject violence."

The way of Jesus is forgiveness, love, and peace. And it's only when we bring the specific contribution of the gospel, the rejection of violence, acceptance of acts of love, that we have been converted— and we will be truly a peace church.

Sullivan: I'll conclude with a sign of hope. I gave a talk in Hampton about a week ago. A man came up to me when I had finished and told me he was an army colonel and that he agreed with everything I had said. Later I got a call from the fort and was invited to meet with three generals, who all happen to be Catholic, to discuss the issues. The colonel said to me on the phone, "I cannot tell you what a contribution you have made. It's the first time in the history of this fort that we are looking at weapons from a moral point of view. You have everybody down here talking."

Witness is just one aspect of the response we must make to the arms race. We should reach out in love and dialogue. I do believe there's a tremendous readiness to listen. I think it's the work of the Spirit.

Nuclear holocaust is five minutes away. But maybe those minutes are the graced moment in which God is speaking to all of humanity. We have no option but to go the way of peace. Maybe God is using this threat to give us the opportunity to recognize our common humanity, to bring us into the one world, the one community, the one family of God.

Jim Wallis: A bishop has a great pastoral responsibility toward the people in his diocese. When bishops make statements such as each of you has, there are reverberations through the personal lives of the people whom you serve. What have been some of the responses and consequences of your witness?

Hunthausen: A gentleman who works at Boeing told me that he and several of his friends customarily arrived early at work to play cards before they went on the job. He said that he and the others haven't played cards since I made my statement. They've been discussing it and the implications in their lives. He was neither happy nor angry, but simply noted that it had forced them to see their personal responsibility, to examine their work and see how closely allied it might be with the nuclear effort.

Most of the letters I've received have been supportive. But some people I've talked to feel a deep fear that all they have worked hard for and acquired will be taken away from them, and they equate that with what they identify as a frivolous statement on my part.

I visit a different parish every weekend, and many people go out of their way to thank me for bringing up the issue. My sense is that my statement has provided a moment of challenge, and that was primarily my purpose—to acquaint people of the diocese with the realization that it is the responsibility of each of us to look at the gospel, examine its implications, and take a personal stance.

Matthiesen: The immediate reaction to my statement came in letters, which varied from calling me a traitor and inviting me to go to Russia and stay there, to thanks for raising my voice in a prophetic way. There was some shock and surprise, and also a lot of confusion.

One woman in our office used to work at the nuclear assembly plant. She said, "I don't know why the bishop made a statement like that; after all, the neutron bomb can destroy buildings and tanks and things, but it doesn't hurt people." And someone said, "I think it's the other way around," and her mouth just fell open. That kind of confusion is very common in our area.

But I detect a definite shift in people's attitudes. The mail is running overwhelmingly in favor of the stand—about 95 percent.

A reporter from an out-of-town newspaper spent several days in Amarillo going into bars and restaurants talking with people. He came to me later and said I would be interested to know that there's a surprising amount of support for my statement out there. Even the people who disagree with my stand are doing it much more reflectively than they did before.

I was thrilled when some of the priests and deacons told me that peace talk is coming from the pulpits everywhere. Those who were concerned about peace have been released to talk about it.

Some of the Catholic people who work at the plant wrote to me and said that they disagreed completely with my stance. They believed that what they were doing was good, and they intended to continue. But I am told that the possibility of resigning is a topic of conversation among the workers.

Wallis: Approximately 10 million Americans earn their livelihood preparing for nuclear war. What about the workers who become convinced of the immorality of their jobs, but have families to care for and feel themselves to be without options? Can you imagine the church becoming a place of sanctuary, providing a pastoral community in which people who want to change their lives can find the economic and spiritual help to do so?

Hunthausen: I have a fund started to help such people. It's not very big yet, and it's a kind of a band-aid business. What if a hundred people needed that fund? Even if six people told me, "I'm leaving my job tomorrow, can you help me?" I don't know what I'd do. I would be forced to appeal to the larger community.

The church has got to take responsibility. It's one thing to talk about the morality of an issue, but we have a responsibility if we're going to urge people to change from the manufacture of military equipment.

Matthiesen: Most people who work at Pantex are not thinking that they are building weapons; they're working for a paycheck. And if we had something else for them to do, they wouldn't mind changing.

In Amarillo there was a big airbase during World War II— 20,000 jet mechanics in training, with support personnel. A tremendous amount of money came into Amarillo as a result. Then it was closed, and I remember the bumper stickers: "Will the last person leaving Amarillo please turn out the lights." But people got together to do something about it, and the facilities were turned into a state institute where they train people in peacetime work. There are any number of like industries there now, and we're much better off than we were before. There are a lot more jobs for the local people.

Hunthausen: I have been invited to an open meeting of three parishes located four miles from the Bangor submarine base. The people there are either in the military or work in connection with it. It is significant that I did not force myself on these people; they invited me, because they want to know what I think.

Wallis: It seems that unless the church takes a leadership role, the prospects of a peace movement, let alone peace, in our country are small. That doesn't mean leadership by control, but by example, by sacrifice, by commitment and risk taking.

Gumbleton: I find most inspiring the fact that each of us here is committed to peace out of religious conviction. I agree that we won't have a genuine peace movement if it is not coming out of a deep faith. People have to be converted.

Mattiesen: We need to be aware that there will be opposition to the things we are saying. That is why we meet together, so that criticism doesn't throw us off our course or make us weak. Together we can make sure that we are ready to suffer, if need be. I'm not asking that we be martyrs, but if this thing catches on we're going to see strong opposition. So the faith basis for it becomes even more important.

Wallis: What do you think it means for the church to commit itself to peace?

Gumbleton: I think some people will be alienated by the changes and that there will be a splitting off; not that we want that to happen, but there will be a challenge to Christian faith.

Hunthausen: On the other hand, some young people have called me who identified themselves as former Catholics. They are now coming back into the church, because for the first time they see the church being relevant.

Matthiesen: The church's commitment to peace is going to create tension. Some will argue that the church should stay out of politics. But if the issue touches people on a faith level, individuals will have to deal with it at the root of their being. They will have to undergo some change in their lives. They will need to examine what that means in their relationship one with the other. It could have tremendous impact on family life if families begin to take seriously the church's doctrines on peace.

39

It is radical, which is the way the church should be. I think if the churches would do what they are called to do in this area, the world has to take it seriously.

Wallis: In the last decade, we have watched with a great deal of hope the conversion of the church in Latin America to the poor. A church that was once part of the ruling powers has become the victim of the same establishment. So by its conversion, the church is having its vocation radicalized. Do you see that happening to the U.S. church in its conversion to peace?

Hunthausen: You scare me. I really don't know, but it seems to me that that's the gospel.

It certainly would be hard for me to accept what was happening in the churches who authentically set out to be a peace church or a church for the poor but were satisfied with power and wealth and vested interests. That's the area where people don't want to be touched. If the church is opposing those interests, we have to expect to suffer some kind of retaliation.

Wallis: You each have spoken in a way that suggests that repentance in a nuclear age means non-cooperation. Would you comment on that and relate it to what you see happening as the church moves toward making a statement on a new position on peace in November, 1982?

Gumbleton: We are clearly committed to changing the present direction of our country's policies. The church has said that nuclear weapons are immoral, and yet we can tolerate this evil in our midst as long as we know that genuine efforts are being made to reduce and finally eliminate such weapons. But we seem not to have made any progress on negotiations. Therefore we can no longer tolerate our country possessing these weapons. It is our right and our responsibility to protest.

Joan Chittister

A Benedictine Prioress

The sign on the front of the display booth in the Pittsburgh airport read: "Build More Nukes. Feed Jane Fonda to the Whales." When I confronted the young man behind the counter in the neat business suit about the callousness of the presentation he explained, patronizingly, "We're only trying to get the liberals to develop a little sense of humor, ma'am."

Later that same month, the Physicians for the Prevention of Nuclear War, Inc., an international organization of doctors, met to begin a campaign intended to build resistance to the design and use of nuclear weapons in the militaries of the world. They were quoted in the January 12, 1981 issue of *Time* as saying:

> How can we dispel the notion of some people that anyone will survive a nuclear war? How can we as doctors influence people to prevent any further buildup of nuclear arms? The medical profession should more actively protest against the senseless policy of increasing arsenals of thermonuclear arms.

A week later, President Jimmy Carter, in his last address to the nation before leaving office, warned:

> The [nuclear] danger is becoming greater. As the arsenals of the superpowers grow in size and sophistication and as other governments—perhaps even, in the future, dozens of governments—acquire these weapons, it may only be a matter of time before madness, desperation, greed or miscalculation lets loose this terrible force . . . the United States and all countries must find ways to control and to reduce the horrifying danger that is posed by the enormous world stockpiles of nuclear arms. . . .

41

All of these positions agitated me. Not because I lack humor; not simply because a president made a statement for what could conceivably have been purely political purposes; not because I'm afraid to die in a nuclear war. On the contrary, I am much more apprehensive about surviving one.

No, the positions affected me because they brought to the surface for one more agonizing time the reality of insanity; mine as well as the nation's. I realized then that I'd been writing this chapter for months—perhaps for years—and the process had been painful, barren, threatening, so delicate a subject. It was not the usual business-as-usual material on ministry or leadership or the standard theology of religious life. This chapter had something to do with me, with my life, with what my very existence is about.

The commitment it reflects has not come easily. It has not, in fact, completely clarified yet. But it is embedded in who I am as Benedictine, as woman, and as educator. On these points, at least, I'm ready now.

As an educator, I am first of all confused and concerned by the language that masked the reality of the nuclear age. To distance ourselves from the unacceptable effects of nuclear annihilation, we use words with acceptable overtones or connotations. We talk about *surgical strike* or precisely targeted attacks, presumably on military installations, as if in a nuclear attack there could really be contained contamination. Americans, of course, feel strongly that anything "surgical" is curative, humanitarian, of lofty purpose. What could possibly be wrong with anything so controlled, so pure of heart? Unless, of course, what is to be excised is a tumor in the brain: Norad in Colorado Springs, for instance; the Pentagon in Washington, D.C.; or Rocky Flats in Denver—all obvious sites of attack in case of nuclear war and all in heavily populated and vital areas; all said now to be able to be removed "surgically."

We fail, in other words, to recognize that even in a so-called strike the "cure" may be as deadly as the disease. The operation may indeed succeed, but the patient will be permanently disabled nevertheless.

"Attack" would be so much more honest a word. The purpose would be clearer; the effects more understandable. Why don't we simply say attack and destroy and annihilate and contaminate; that is what we are really prepared to do.

When I discovered that "collateral damage" was military terminology for the civilian deaths to be expected in nuclear conflict, I realized how far away we've strayed from our consciousness or care of human life no matter what our national self-image might be. People had become "units of loss" rather than names or personalities or family figures. People had become tallies on our war-game charts whose destruction we figure with pride.

I began to cringe at the comedic acronyms—SAINT, HALO, BAMBI—we were using to make the sinister—the satanic perhaps—benign characters in the national fairy tale. Only one, MAD—Mutually Assured Destruction—a term used to describe our ability to retaliate with equally incapacitating force—signaled the psychotic state of the nation and my own contribution to it.

I began to resent the scientific jargon that made the military scrabble game a tower of nationalist Babel. The widow next door, the high school senior, the welder of car fenders, the hard-hat brick layer know about security and freedom and the Halls of Montezuma and Gettysburg. On the other hand they may not really understand that behind the high-sounding technological gobbledeygook— ICBM, B-1 bomber, MX missile system, megatons—lies hair-trigger weaponry capable of wiping out entire cities of people like themselves. They are, however, certainly awed and impressed into accepting silence by the cold complexities of these titles.

I began to suspect the talk about nuclear "defense" that acknowledged all the while that the only way to defend oneself from nuclear destruction was to strike first. Someone will have to judge when that has become necessary, which means that we are prepared to strike first and be wrong. But I began to see, too, that the country that strikes first will have nothing left to claim, that the entire world economy could collapse as a result, that first-strike nations will strike themselves at the same time.

The madness began to be too, too plain to me; my too common common sense began to wither.

And then I realized that the people are not meant to understand. Because, though simple people want to defend their own security and lives, they really do not, most of them, really want to take anyone else's—not massively, not indiscriminately, not savagely. And the language solves that. What can be savage that is so scientific? Long ago the doable became the desirable in the Western world; long ago technology became God and the schizophrenic language of science its liturgy.

As an educator I began to know that it is not that we are so close to a nuclear mind-set that had begun to bother me. It is that, despite its ominous and general presence, we are so far away from it: twenty-year-olds sit at the bottom of missile silos with their fingers over launch buttons while a world that can already destroy itself once stockpiles to do it one hundred times. They will never see the faces of their victims, never watch civilian babies die, never see the world's farm lands shrivel. They will never have to see the consequences of their actions. They will simply know that they have been "surgical," "innocent," "scientific."

I have found myself, in other words, in the long struggle to understand the nuclear issue hardened by its language, diminished by its distance, lied to. As an educator I had come to a dead end. "Thy speech hath betrayed thee" rang in my ears.

But there were even deeper dimensions to my developing consciousness. I was a Benedictine and a woman. I had to ask myself in the face of these realities what it now meant to be both.

To be Benedictine was the most burdensome blessing of all. The monastic life had long been defined as ascetic, other-worldly, withdrawn. Good monks and nuns—the 19th-century understanding went—were to struggle to transcend an evil world, to remove themselves from its secular concerns, to be above the interests or problems of their times. Gone for ages was the memory of the monastery as the center of the city; of the monastic as leader and leaven.

To be Benedictine and monastic no longer meant to see what others were not sensitive to; to do what others had not done; to cry gospel in a guarded world. The monastic life had become pious, passive, and protected. Separation of church and state brought us to the point where it was now considered sacrilegious for the Christian to call the conscience of the king.

We were a long way from the social and pacifist tradition that was basic to the Benedictine life and the church from which it sprung.

But I knew that it had been monastic communities which in earlier times had taken personal responsibility for the shaping of human community. This Benedictine posture was evident through centuries of disease, poverty, and public calamity. Intervening to assert the right of all to share in the wealth of God's creation, monasteries organized relief before state agencies existed. During the time of usurious lending, Benedictines established a system of monastic mortgages with loans at reasonable rates, and gave interest-free loans to aid victims of natural catastrophe. Hospitality extended to nobles, prisoners, indigents, social outcasts, and slaves.

And I remembered that in his *Life of Antony,* Athanasius had written of that monk's confrontation with the civil system:

> When the judge saw the fearlessness of Antony and of those with him, he issued the order that none of the monks were to appear in the law court, nor were they to stay in the city at all. All the others thought it was wise to go into hiding that day, but Antony took this so seriously as to wash his upper garment and to stand the next day in a prominent place in front and to be clearly visible to the prefect. When, while all marveled at this, the prefect, passing by with his escort, saw him, he stood there calmly, demonstrating the purposefulness that belongs to us Christians.

I was moved to admit that there had been no room in my own religious formation for these kinds of witness.

I realized, too, that from the earliest centuries, both monks and clerics had claimed exemption from military service on the grounds that those who were intent on modeling the Christ-life simply could not kill. I became keenly aware that Benedictines' most ancient motto was Pax; that Benedictines had provided sanctuary during the medieval wars; that the Benedictine Order was credited with having once saved Western civilization. I became convinced that the kind of leadership brought by Benedictines to the framing of the Truce of God and the Peace of God during the wars of the Middle Ages was needed again in our own time.

To be monastic, I began to think, was to have burning eyes and a prophet's steel voice. As Benedictine I was compelled to face the nuclear issue. But if to be Benedictine in the nuclear age was decisive in my commitment to nuclear disarmament, to be a woman was determinative.

In the nuclear arms race, I saw all the male values of the society run amok. Competition, profit, and power have all conspired to bring the world to the edge of its own destruction. Like bullies on the block the world has gathered its gangs to fight to the death to protect what they don't have a right to in the first place.

Who is best and who is right and who is richest have become

the questions of the human race. Universal political, economic, and social issues are being deterred in their resolution by military threat: macho, pure macho.

Nurturance and imagination are needed; openness and compassion are missing; trust and vulnerability we lack. The feminine view of the world has too long been disregarded.

As a woman whose life has been often predicated on patriarchal norms, I realized that I had had enough of all that. Because the economy depends on the military industry; because the Army wants destructive power to rival the Navy's; because we want to be on top are not reasons I now find compelling. Lesser values are not good enough any more.

G. K. Chesterton once wrote: "It is not that Christianity has been tried and found wanting. Christianity has not been tried."

We are surely at the point where we must all try again, together.

It is out of these perspectives that all the arguments for the arms race fall away. If the Russians were really coming, they could—by our own calculations—easily have come by now. If deterrence is the issue we can, by our own calculations, already destroy the world a hundred times. Isn't once enough?

In the face of this irreparable damage and total destruction, I remember another holocaust and Elie Wiesel's indictment: "And the world was silent." I remember that people were silent as 10,000 people a day were methodically destroyed: six million Jews, one million Jewish children; in the name of someone's national ideals.

Now they say, "No one will ever use nuclear weapons; that's exactly why we build them." But we did. WE did.

I remember too that now we can eliminate, contaminate, erase a culture just as easily as the Nazis exterminated the Jews. I know, in fact, that we plan to do so if and when we decide that it's necessary. I know we call it "surgical strike": methodical, calculated, idealistic.

I was there when Elie Wiesel threw back in our religious faces the final challenge: "If the victim is my problem then the killer is yours. I must ask why Jews walked silently, docilely to their deaths. You must ask how a Christian could murder Jews—one million Jewish children—and remain a Christian. You must ask why no Pope ever excommunicated them."

Elie Wiesel, a Jewish writer and survivor of the German

death-camps at Auschwitz and Birchenau, is intent on reminding people what it is to exterminate a nation. He is keeping the memory of the horror alive in this generation so that another age does not repeat the barbarism. Elie Wiesel is trying to make us confront this era's sin of silence.

As educator, as Benedictine, as woman, I fear this generation's sin of silence.

Glen Stassen

A Southern Baptist Theologian

I am a Baptist, a Southern Baptist. If I am to write of my personal pilgrimage into peacemaking, honesty requires that I write both about the experience of the mushroom cloud and about the experience of conversion and commitment, baptism, and the lordship of Christ.

I was only six years old when my father went to the South Pacific to fight in the Navy during World War II, but I did what I could to support the war effort. Knowing that if the Japanese came to attack us, they would come across the ocean, and knowing that oceangoing vessels could come within a stone's throw of our home alongside the Mississippi River, I dug a foxhole on the hillside, gathered some stones, and found a garbage can lid to use as a shield so I'd be ready when they came. I formed a club to collect scrap metal, modestly naming it "Glen's Bravados." I grew a victory garden full of carrots, white radishes, and cut worms; we ate the carrots and radishes, thus helping the war effort.

After awhile the letters from my father stopped coming. From another family in our town, whose son was in my father's fleet, we learned that Dad's ship had been torpedoed and sunk. Then a naval officer called to ask whether he could come to our home to speak with my mother. We knew he was coming to tell us Dad had been killed in action. While we waited for him to come, we cried the uncontrollable and unshareable tears that too many families of too many nations during too many wars have cried.

For us that wrenching sorrow lasted only half a day; the officer had not thought to tell my mother that he only wanted to discuss some minor business and fill out some forms. Only later did we learn my father had been rescued and was alive. Although our momentary but intense sorrow was nothing compared to what millions have had to suffer, it gave us a glimpse of the awful pain and tragedy of war, and an awareness that war is not a remote possibility or a remote event; war does happen, and does come home to real families.

When I was nine, we received the news that two atomic bombs had been exploded on the families living in Hiroshima and Nagasaki. The killing caused by those bombs, and their portent for a future threatened with global nuclear war against *all* families, came home to me especially because my father was over there, and because later he showed us pictures of the war-caused suffering. I had something like a vision, though not a "strange" vision with mystical secrets; it was simply a very clear mental picture of a mushroom cloud, a clear awareness that the cloud threatened human life for all of us, and a knowledge that we must take some action to stop nuclear war from happening. I can remember exactly where I was sitting, and I can remember that I felt called, that we were all called, to do something new and imaginative to get that mushroom cloud under control.

When I was eleven, my cousin, Ronald Erickson, brought me with him to a revival meeting at our church. The sermon described how God has demonstrated powerful love for us by entering into our human situation, coming in the form of a humble servant and living among us, even to the point of suffering and dying on the cross. I remember this event vividly, too—just where we were sitting, the central theme of the sermon, and how I felt called to respond to this love and to commit myself to follow Christ and live in Christlike love. I responded to that call.

My pastor, John Wobig, then did far more for my becoming a Christian than he knows. Instead of putting me in a class and telling me what the church believes and what church membership means for a Baptist, he met with me individually in his office several times and asked all sorts of probing and guiding questions about the meaning of the commitment I was making, about the meaning of baptism for me, about Jesus, God, faith, forgiveness, love, and other dimensions of my growing commitment.

He helped me begin my Christian life not as a passive listener but as an active witnesser. It was a moment of *kairos* for me. It deepened, strengthened, and clarified my own personal commitment, and helped make my subsequent baptism a continuously life-shaping event. It has given much impetus and direction to whatever peacemaking I have done.

And so the vision of the mushroom cloud and the experience of conversion and baptism became permanent ingredients of my pilgrimage—or my wanderings. The dialogue between them took place first as I worked through the question of vocation. Although at that early age I had no idea what my vocation would be, I was clear then that conversion and baptism meant all of life comes under the lordship of Christ, no matter what one's vocation turns out to be.

Therefore, when it turned out that my talents were in physics, mathematics, logic, and puzzle-solving rather than in the use of words, I plunged into nuclear physics as my Christian vocation.

At the University of Virginia some of my excellent professors of physics had helped in building the atomic bomb. At the Naval Research Laboratory, I worked assisting Dr. James Butler in his skillful use of the Van de Graff accelerator to probe the mysterious infinitesimal depths of the nucleus. Then I got a better-paying job (to pay for getting married), drawing up wiring diagrams for the electronics in the Air Force's Distant Early Warning Line (DEW line), which was to warn us when the Russian bombers would come over the North Pole. We constructed a DEW line so proficient that it announced the Russians were coming when the full moon rose, and again when a flock of geese flew across Canada. Fortunately *then* there was no incentive to launch a quick, irreversible counterattack based only on electronic warnings. Bombers were slow and could be called back, unlike the quick-trigger missile systems both superpowers are now planning to build.

The more I became involved in my studies and work, the more clearly I saw the trends of the future. It did not require the genius of an Einstein or the sensitivity of the prophet Jeremiah to see that we were headed toward ever-increasing probability of the use of nuclear weapons. It did not take advanced calculus to know that if we keep playing nuclear roulette year after year, the cumulative probability of a megadeath outcome gets larger and larger.

For me it meant a switch in vocation. I saw that humankind was in an emergency situation, in great need, heading toward ever-increasing indescribable danger. To respond to the love of God revealed in Christ means to respond to need by entering into the situation and participating in the way of deliverance. It seemed clear to me that we already had abundant talent developing nuclear technology, and that I should do what little I could to work on controlling that technology.

And so I headed to seminary and graduate school, and became a teacher of Christian ethics specializing in implications of the Christian faith for peace and war and the nuclear arms race, but also working on other issues such as theological ethics, methodology, and racial justice. My confession of sin is that I have known far better the conflict between the lordship of Christ and the meaning of the trends of the nuclear arms race than I have written. For this I have been repenting.

One reason for this new repentance is the objective trend of the nuclear arms race. I had foreseen the increasing danger of holocaust, but not the kinds of weapons the two superpowers would plan for the 1980's: weapons 15 times as powerful as the Hiroshima bomb but too small and concealable to be verified and controlled by mutual agreement; weapons so accurate, numerous, and quick that they threaten to destroy the other side's missiles in a quick first-strike, thus pushing the other side to fire at a moment's possibly false warning; and weapons based on the ground in a few storage areas within eight minutes of the other side.

Furthermore, it has now become clear that the United States and the Soviet Union have not used the time they have had and the negotiations that many of us have urged to get the weapons under control.

My understanding of the fallenness of the principalities and powers, out from whose lordship we have been baptized, requires my strategy to be both independent and critical of the government. At the same time, I know the authorities are charged under Christ to serve peace and justice, and therefore I am required to be constructive in pushing the government to take initiatives to make peace. And *that* requires political and technical analyses with Christian ethical criteria.

A second reason for my new repentance is a new and special sense of community among peacemakers in Louisville, at the Southern Baptist Theological Seminary, and in the Southern Baptist Convention. Something new is happening among Southern Baptists, and it is related to the experience of lordship of Christ over all of life.

At our annual conventions, large majorities have passed

strong resolutions on the nuclear arms race and mutual arms reduction, world hunger, and human rights. Conservative and moderate leaders have joined in supporting a Southern Baptist convocation on the nuclear arms race and urging President Reagan to speak out on human rights. The Christian Life Commission, the Brotherhood, the Home Mission Board, and Church Training are publishing materials on peacemaking. Two Southern Baptist newspapers, *SEEDS* and *The Baptist Peacemaker,* are being published with rapidly increasing circulation, and peacemaker groups as well as hunger groups are being formed in an increasing number of churches.

To understand Southern Baptist peacemaking efforts one must remember our experience of struggle, conversion, and commitment in the process of emancipation from the old chains of segregation and discrimination that had shackled our pulpits and our lives. The gospel was locked into a compartment of inner conversion, love toward individuals, and future salvation. Meanwhile another standard ruled over our outer conformism, embarrassed injustice, and defense of a romanticized past. Nor can we claim all is under his lordship now. But the barrier is down. Apparently Billy Graham is an example of this. He has begun warning that "a nuclear holocaust . . . is almost certainly inevitable if the arms race is not stopped," and emphasizes that "God is concerned about every area of life, and Christ's lordship means we also must be concerned about every area of our lives and seek to bring everything under that lordship."

My own biblical studies have led me to the prophets, who not only describe Isaiah's famous hope for beating swords into plowshares, but diagnose the major causes of war as injustice and idolatry, and call for practical action—repentance for idolatry and compassionate justice for the oppressed.

In the New Testament, the Sermon on the Mount does not so much tell us to *refrain* from doing violence, as call us to take practical, surprising initiatives in order to create peaceful community: go talk to your brother or sister and be reconciled, turn the other cheek (a surprising initiative, not merely a refraining from retaliation), carry your enemy's pack two miles (reconciling as you go), give to the poor who beg (feeding the hungry), love your enemies and pray for them.

I have been drawn to Paul's letters, especially Romans, which I was surprised to observe begin and end by praying both for grace and for peace, and emphasize practical peacemaking throughout— something I had not been taught.

And I have noted that Revelation does not teach the idolatrous belief that our future depends on our building more nuclear weapons than the Russians, but on our obeying the teachings of Jesus and following the Lamb. Revelation, too, is a practical book. It repeatedly points the way to take toward peace in a time of heavy threat: follow the commandments of the Lamb.

My own peacemaker group has studied what steps we could take. We took initiatives to encourage our own church and other churches in our city and state to pray for peace. Among many other activities, we have written letters, made phone calls, and gathered petitions. We actively support and participate in the Louisville Council on Peacemaking and Religion. We helped sponsor a Kentucky Pastors Conference on Peacemaking in our church.

This Louisville group and the recent events in the wider Southern Baptist community have profoundly shaped my understanding of peacemaking. Many have experienced through struggle and conversion a new dedication to the lordship of Christ over all of life. I believe we are called not simply to produce pious statements, but to participate in practical action to get the mushroom cloud under control.

John R. W. Stott

An Anglican Clergyman

Converted to Jesus Christ two months before my seventeenth birthday, and 18 months before the outbreak of World War II, I was an immediate and instinctive pacifist. The Jesus who had entered my life and become real to me was the same Jesus who had said, "Do not resist one who is evil," "if any one strikes you on the right cheek, turn to him the other also," and again, "love your enemies, and pray for those who persecute you" (Matthew 5:39, 44). How then could I, in the first flush of a disciple's devotion to his Lord, contemplate reversing his instructions? How could I hate and retaliate and strike and kill? The very possibility was inconceivable to me. So, having signified my desire to be ordained before hostilities began, I was able to apply for exemption from military service, and was granted it.

As the years passed, as my knowledge of the Bible grew, and with it my desire to balance Scripture with Scripture, I began to see that the issue was not as clearcut as I had at first imagined. I learned that one reason why we Christians are not to repay evil with evil or to avenge ourselves is that we are to "leave it to the wrath of God," of whom it is written "vengeance is mine, I will repay, says the Lord" (Romans 12:17–19); and that one means by which this "wrath" and "vengeance" of God against evil are expressed is through the judicial processes of the state, which is "God's servant" with authority from God to use force to bring offenders to justice (Romans 13:1–5).

The only way I could see to resolve this tension between the teaching of Romans and of the Sermon on the Mount was to distinguish between the respective duties of the individual Christian (to forbear retaliation, to love, to forgive, to pray and to do good) and of the state (to avenge evil by the administration of justice). More-

54

over, in some situations it seemed to me legitimate—and not incompatible with Scripture—that the police should be supplemented and even replaced by soldiers to accomplish this task. Yet the essence of this kind of police action was its *discriminate* nature. Indiscriminate violence was inexcusable; the state's use of force could be justified only in the strictly discriminating task of bringing particular criminals to justice. Maybe, I thought, this principle might just be extended to include a very small number of wider conflicts or wars.

But now in my thinking the pendulum has swung again, as I take note of the appallingly indiscriminate nature of atomic weapons. The contemporary buildup of the superpowers' nuclear arsenals is a horrendous reality. The nuclear warheads of the United States alone could annihilate the complete world population 12 times over. What is this lunacy?

Five nations are now known to have both nuclear weapons and delivery systems, while five more have the capability to develop them. The Stockholm International Peace Research Institute (SIPRI) forecasts that, by 1985, the nuclear club may have grown to 35 member nations. Already some $800,000 a minute are being spent on "defense." How can one correlate this with the 800 million people who are said to be destitute? As Eisenhower expressed it, "Every gun made is a theft from the hungry."

Nobody can predict with any accuracy how much devastation a nuclear war would cause. But the U.S. Congress document *The Effects of Nuclear War* (1979) says that "the minimum consequences would be enormous." It provides four case-studies ranging from a single megaton weapon attack on a city the size of Detroit or Leningrad to "a very large attack against a range of military and economic targets" in which the USSR struck first and the U.S. retaliated. The former would mean up to two million dead; the latter would mean up to 77 percent of the American population (160 million) and up to 40 percent of the Russian population would be killed. Moreover, these casualties would be due to the immediate blast wave, fire storm, and direct radiation. Many more millions would later die of their injuries, or starve or freeze to death the following winter; in the long term, cancer would claim yet more victims, and the genetic and ecological consequences would be incalculable.

It is against this background of horror that we need to hear again the words of Jesus: *Blessed are the peacemakers, for they shall be called God's children.* Peacemaking has the blessing and approval of God because it is a divine activity, and we can claim to be authentic children of God only if we seek to do what our Heavenly Father is doing. Thus, the basis for peacemaking is theological: It derives from our doctrine of God.

To be sure, the God of the Bible is a God of both salvation and judgment. But not equally so, as if these were parallel expressions of his nature. For Scripture called judgment his "strange work"; his characteristic work, in which he delights, is salvation or peacemaking. Similarly, Jesus reacted to willful perversity with anger, uttered scathing denunciations upon hypocrites, drove the moneychangers out of the temple and overturned their tables. But he also endured the humiliation and barbarities of flogging and crucifixion without resistance. Thus we see in the ministry of the same Jesus both violence and nonviolence. Yet his resort to violence of word and deed was occasional, alien, uncharacteristic; his characteristic was nonviolence; the symbol of his ministry is not the whip but the cross.

It is on the ground of this theology—of this revelation of God in Christ and in Scripture—that we Christians must all be opposed to war and dedicated to peace. Of course, throughout the centuries different Christians have formulated their conclusions differently. Some have been total pacifists, arguing that the example and teaching of Jesus commit his disciples to renounce the use of force in any form and to follow instead the way of the cross, that is, of nonviolent love. Others have emphasized that officers of the state are "ministers of God" appointed to reward good conduct and punish bad, have argued that Christian citizens may share in the state's God-given role, and have sought to extend it into the international arena in terms of the "just war." Although this notion has been expressed in various forms, it may be said to have at least four essential aspects.

First, the cause must be righteous. That is, the war must be defensive not aggressive, its goal must be to secure justice and peace, and it may be justified only as a last resort after all attempts at reconciliation have failed.

Second, the means must be controlled. Two key words have been used regarding the limitation of violence. One is "proportionate." That is, the degree of injury inflicted must be less than that incurred. The other word is "discriminate." Proper police action is essentially discriminate, namely the arresting, bringing to trial, and punishment of specific criminals. Similarly, a war could not be in any sense "just" unless directed only against enemy combatants, leaving civilians immune.

This principle is enough to condemn the saturation bombing of German cities in World War II (as Bishop George Bell of Chichester had the courage to argue in the House of Lords); and the fact that Hitler started it is no excuse. I myself believe that the same principle is sufficient to condemn the use of strategic nuclear weapons. Because they are indiscriminate in their effects, destroying combatants and noncombatants alike, it seems clear to me that nuclear weapons are ethically indefensible, and that every Christian, whatever he or she may think of the possibility of a "just" use of conventional weapons, must be a nuclear pacifist.

Third, the motive must be pure, for in no circumstances whatever does Christianity tolerate hatred, cruelty, envy, or greed. And fourth, the outcome must be predictable. That is, there must be a reasonable prospect of victory, and so of gaining the just ends for which the war is fought.

My point, however, is not so much to weigh the respective arguments that some adduce for total pacifism and others for the "just war" position, but rather to emphasize that the advocates of *both* positions are opposed to war. So then, although "just war" proponents may seek to justify engagement in war in certain restricted circumstances, they should never seek to glorify it. They may acquiesce in it with the greatest reluctance and the most painful qualms of conscience, but only if they perceive it as the least of all the alternative evils. Although we should honor those who conscientiously fight and die for the defense of their country, we should steadfastly refuse to glamorize war. War remains inhuman, unChristian, bestial. It is peacemaking we are to glorify. But what can it mean to be a Christian peacemaker amid the frightening realities of the nuclear age?

First, *Christian peacemakers must recover their morale.* There is a tendency among today's church members either to grow so accustomed to the balance of terror that we lose our sense of outrage, or to become so pessimistic that we acquiesce in it with a feeling of helplessness. But indifference and pessimism are inappropriate, even inadmissible, in Christians. To give up either feeling or hoping is to have parted company with Jesus Christ. We need to recover our sense of shame and indignation over the arms race, and to resolve to join others in seeking to reverse it.

Second, *Christian peacemakers must be more diligent in prayer.* I beg you not to dismiss this statement as a piece of pietistic irrelevance. For Christian believers, it is nothing of the sort. Irrespective of the rationale and the efficacy of prayer, we are under orders. Jesus our Lord specifically commanded us to pray for our enemies: do we? Paul laid down as the first duty of every gathered congregation, the responsibility to pray for their national leaders, so that "we may lead a quiet and peaceable life" (1 Timothy 2:1, 2). He thus attributed peace to prayer. Today virtually every church has a period of intercession in its public worship. Supposing the whole church family were, during this period, to unite in fervent, concentrated prayer for rulers, for enemies, for peace, freedom, and justice in the world, what might God not do in response to his people's humble petitions?

Third, *Christian peacemakers must supply an example of a community peace.* It is impossible for Christians to maintain a credible witness for peace in the world unless the church is itself seen to be a community of peace. If charity begins at home, so does reconciliation. We need to obey the teaching of Jesus that we *first* be reconciled to our brother and sister and *then* come and offer our worship (Matthew 5:23, 24). We need to forgive our enemies, mend our broken relationships, ensure that our homes are havens of love, joy, and peace, and banish from our church all malice, anger, and bitterness.

God's purpose, through the work of his Son and his Spirit, is to create a new, reconciled society. He means his church to be a sign of his kingdom, that is, a model of what human community looks like when it comes under his gracious rule. He wants his new community to challenge the value system of the secular community, and to offer a viable alternative, attractive because it is authentic. Not that this is easy. Peace is not a synonym for appeasement. God's own peacemaking involved the blood of the cross; true Christian peacemaking is painful and costly too.

Fourth, *Christian peacemakers must contribute to confidence building.* There has been a lot of study of the postures of aggression that individual human beings adopt when they feel threatened. But not enough study has been done on the behavior of states under

threat, that is, on the psychology of national aggression. Have you ever asked yourself how much Soviet behavior (in the buildup of its arsenal) may be aggressive not so much because it is ambitious for power as because it feels threatened? How far could its aggressive stance be a sign not of imperialism, but of insecurity?

We must agree that each of the two superpowers perceives the other as a threat, and that Christians should support any means to reduce this confrontation of mutual suspicion and fear. The Helsinki Final Act (1975) spoke of "confidence building measures" whose purpose was to remove the fear of sudden attack and develop reciprocal trust. The kind of measures in view were the establishment of demilitarized buffer zones, advance notification of military maneuvers, the exchange of information and observers, and verification measures to enforce arms control agreements.

It seems to me, however, that there is also scope for the development of Christian confidence building measures. I understand that the Mennonite Central Committee arranges student exchanges between the U.S. and both Poland and East Germany. Ought not Christian travel agencies to organize more tour groups to visit the Soviet Union? It is reliably reported that, despite more than 60 years of atheistic propaganda, still between 15 and 20 percent of Russians are church members. Yet the links between Western and Russian Christians are minimal. A strengthening of this fellowship could be influential in breaking down caricatures, allaying fears, and spreading trust.

Fifth, *Christian peacemakers must promote more public debate.* Questions need to be asked. Could it ever be justifiable to buy national defense at the cost of millions of civilian lives? Does not the Bible roundly condemn "the shedding of innocent blood," and do not nuclear weapons come under this condemnation? Is not national morality in the end more important than national security?

In promoting public debate of the ethical issues, Christians need at the same time to be realistic. The call for immediate, total, unilateral nuclear disarmament seems to me unrealistic. Christians could, however, call for a unilateral gesture of disarmament, as an example of the "audacious gestures of peace" that Pope John Paul II has canvassed. I believe we should call on our governments to declare at least a temporary moratorium on the development and testing of all new nuclear weapons systems, and then wait for a complementary, balancing move from the other side. Such a bold initiative might break the deadlock and begin to reverse the arms race.

In my view, however, the most dramatic of all confidence building measures would be for each nuclear power to make an unequivocal, unilateral, public pledge that it will under no circumstances be the first to use a strategic nuclear weapon. Unfortunately, the possibility of such a pledge has become less likely in the last decade because of the American decision to develop the long-range, highly accurate cruise missile, the Pentagon's policy change to a counterforce strategy, and subsequently President Carter's Directive 59, which discarded deterrence by the threat of a retaliatory, second strike and authorized instead a first, preemptive strike on Soviet missile sites. This was a dangerously provocative step, which was bound in itself to increase Soviet fears and, in the event of use, would inevitably escalate into full-scale nuclear war, the ultimate apocalypse. By contrast, the simple, single act of publicly and permanently renouncing the first-strike tactic would immediately defuse the current explosive situation and cool the international climate.

Of course, we shall not succeed in building a utopia of peace and plenty on earth. Jesus said, "There will be wars and rumors of wars." Not till he returns will all swords be beaten into plowshares and spears into pruning hooks. But this fact cannot be made an excuse for building sword and spear factories. Does Christ's prediction of famine inhibit us from feeding the hungry and seeking a more equitable distribution of food? No more can his prediction of wars inhibit us from seeking peace. God is a peacemaker. If we want to qualify as God's authentic children, we must be peacemakers too.

Molly Rush

A Grandmother and Activist

The bare bones are these, in reverse order of occurrence: grandmother; convicted felon awaiting appeal on a two- to five-year jail sentence; director of a peace and justice ministry since 1973; mother of four sons and two daughters, aged twenty-seven to fourteen; wife of Bill for twenty-eight years; eldest of eight children of Dave and Mary Moore.

In looking back, I see continuity and struggle, a struggle that continues as I ponder the future in terms of responsibility and, especially, of hope. Today I know hope as a lived experience, not as a choice or a false optimism. For that I am deeply grateful.

The crimes for which I was convicted are defined differently by the courts than by me and my friends, now called the Plowshares Eight. In choosing to call forth hope by disarming two Mark 12A nuclear warheads which, when armed, could each cause more innocent deaths and suffering than a Dachau or a Buchenwald, we believe we were acting both legally and morally. It was a response to a legal system that serves to protect the production of genocidal weapons and thereby threatens the life of each child now living and generations not yet born.

As I await the birth of my second grandchild, I know that today the world is a more dangerous place than it was on September 9, 1980, when we walked into that General Electric plant in King of Prussia, Pennsylvania, where these warheads are produced on an assembly line. In taking hammers to the lovingly constructed cones of death, then pouring our blood on them, we were engaged in an old biblical task: smashing idols, symbolically turning swords into plowshares.

My desire in taking this action was to break free of the paralyzing power over our lives that these seemingly invulnerable weapons have held, freeing up the possibility for hope in a seemingly

61

hopeless situation. It allowed me to look forward to this child of my child with a sure knowledge that life itself is a miracle and that it is only by letting go of the illusion of control over my life and trusting in the Creator, and not in the bomb, that I can live in hope.

People sometimes look at me in disbelief when I talk of hope as the central reality in my life. With the bomb over all of our heads and a jail sentence over mine, I know that a few years ago I couldn't have talked this way of faith or miracles. I was at best an optimistic pessimist, a somewhat cynical pragmatist, a "realist," I would have said. I had experienced firsthand the injustice of the system and wanted to change it.

Thirty years ago, after hearing my mother talk of trust in God, accepting our cross as God's will, I had decided that attitude was too passive for me. I thought that to accept it meant to accept a fate that should be struggled against. My family had had to go on welfare when my father's drinking had led to the loss of his last job when I was sixteen. I was angry with him and with my mother for putting up with him. I was even angrier at the intrusive questions put to me by a caseworker a few years older than myself, who in different circumstances might have been my friend.

In later years, Mother humorously taped a tiny snapshot of Dad on the back of a pendant that said, "When life gives you lemons, make lemonade." One of her favorite sayings was that we all have a cross to bear. She was no martyr, but a serene and patient woman whose quiet faith sustained her. But I didn't want to hear about crosses.

She would put a good-morning prayer on the bathroom mirror. Above the kitchen sink was a more homey one, "Dear Lord of the pots and pans. . . ." For years I was allergic to pious talk. Yet any vision I had of church was filtered through the example I saw in my mother's life, just as my sense of being Irish was connected to my dad's storytelling, his sense of humor, and his fine Irish tenor voice.

He loved to argue politics, and years later, when I was involved in the civil rights struggle, he would make an outrageous comment just to get me shouting. Then he would tilt back in his chair, laughing delightedly. He had won; a good lesson for a self-righteous new activist.

I inherited his Irish temper. Any patience I've gained was learned from my mother. She always found time to read a story or play a game with the little ones, her joy. The fact that my father didn't work much meant that he had more time for us than most fathers. After I married at nineteen, my brothers and sisters took their turn supporting the younger ones.

I just wanted a husband, home, and children, with a measure of economic stability. By the time I was twenty-six, we had four children, two boys and two girls.

I joined Christian Mothers in the parish where I'd attended grade school and where my mother had once been a member. A black priest came to speak to us about civil rights, my first direct contact with this issue. I had read about the civil rights movement and watched on television the lunch counter sit-ins in which young black people responded nonviolently to having ketchup poured on their heads. I was outraged that a country that guaranteed liberty and justice for all could allow Jim Crow to exist. I wanted a better world and wanted to be part of the movement for change.

When a few people came to my parish to leaflet for Catholic Interracial Council (CIC), I decided to join. I didn't know a single political activist and was timid about joining the NAACP, but this was a step I could take. On my first picket line, in support of the struggle to open craft unions to blacks, a dignified lady approached me as I carried my CIC sign nervously aloft: "Young woman, I'm ashamed to be a Catholic!"

It was not hard to get cynical about the Church when CIC encountered wide opposition in its attempts to desegregate Catholic schools and encourage fair hiring practices within institutions and parishes. The response of the Church to the widening war in Vietnam was also disillusioning. Dr. King had risked broad support for civil rights when he criticized the war, but with the exception of a few priest friends in CIC, the local Catholic church remained silent.

One Sunday, a few people from a group then called Clergy and Laymen Concerned About Vietnam decided to leaflet my parish church. I joined them, four or five people with a poster and some leaflets questioning the morality of the war. My pastor called the local police, and we were faced with arrest if we did not leave. Unprepared for this stunning response, we left.

By this time, my oldest son Gary was entering his teens. My brother Ed, sent to Vietnam as an army cook, had found himself guarding an ammunition dump his first week there. I had written him to say I was marching against the war and to tell him why. He understood. As the war continued, I worried that Gary would reach eighteen and be drafted. I had not raised him to be a soldier.

My husband supported my protests, but devoted most of his energy to softball. He managed a team as a sideline, and it was taking more and more of his time. I continued to work for civil rights. Two sons, Bob and Greg, were born in 1966 and 1968. With the older children in school, the little ones often accompanied me to meetings or marches. I also shared childcare with a friend.

As the war dragged on, several of us formed a group called CEASE in order to raise the issue as Catholics. Shortly afterwards, in 1972, Larry Kessler, Father Jack O'Malley, and I attended a major antiwar conference in Ann Arbor. It was my first overnight stay away from my family except to have a baby. While there, we met Vietnam Veterans Against the War who graphically described their experiences, including their participation in atrocities. We came home with a greater sense of urgency than ever about the need for a full-time peace center. With a few others, we made calls and raised enough pledges of monthly donations to begin.

The Thomas Merton Center opened its doors in March 1973. Larry quit his job to work as director. By the following year, three sisters had been released by their communities to work full time in our justice and peace ministry. Larry was leaving for Boston, and he asked me to take over. Greg was in kindergarten by now, so I became part-time director. We felt it was important to have lay leadership. I expected it to be a short-term commitment, thinking that once the war was over, support would evaporate.

My work with the center was an intense learning experience for me. I began to study world hunger and its causes in order to help develop a slideshow. As I learned of the links between corporate policies of growing export crops on peasant lands and of support for military dictatorships to maintain control of land and resources, and of food aid being sent to Vietnam in order to support the war, I began to understand that hunger and war and other issues such as racism and sexism were linked.

I was meeting people in liberation struggles in Latin America and Africa. Concerns that had once seemed remote became immediate and personal. I was also gaining information on the arms race, learning about MIRVs and MARVs and ICBMs and about the relentless development of weapons systems and policies that were bringing us to the brink of nuclear war. I began to take my concerns home. Would my children even have a future?

I was also learning how to educate and involve people. I saw the church mainly as a vehicle for reaching the people in the pews and helping them to become aware and active. When I read Thomas Merton, I was most likely to choose his writings on peace and social justice. I was inspired by the witness of people such as Daniel and Philip Berrigan, whose nonviolent resistance to the war seemed to come from the same wellsprings of inspiration as had Martin Luther King, Jr.'s. I began to read Gandhi and, later, James Douglass's *The Nonviolent Cross*. Now I was beginning to link my unspoken faith much more directly to my work for justice.

I had friends who had been arrested, but I didn't see myself as ready or able to take such a step. With six kids? Yet, as early as 1973, I remember talking with a nun friend, Marcia Snowden, who spent a week in jail during the Harrisburg conspiracy trial. I remember saying that it shouldn't be only priests and nuns who took these risks, or young men facing the draft. I felt I had all the more reason to protest what I saw as threats to my children's lives, and all the more responsibility. Yet I held back.

For one thing, my mother was operated on and found to have pancreatic cancer about two years after my father's death in 1971. For the next five years, until her death in April 1978, I watched her struggle with a disease I dreaded. I watched her go down to less than half her previous weight, enduring pain, treatments, and operations with quiet grace and courage. I'd bring the children to visit and ask how she was doing. She would say, "Fine," her eyes dancing. She remained herself throughout her five-year illness. I felt she had conquered cancer even as she died in her own bed, holding my hand.

She had never held a job until she was in her late fifties. Raising children was her life. Yet she encouraged and supported my work, no matter how controversial. She was an obedient daughter of the church, yet she gave the final blessing at a prayer service sponsored by our group which supported the ordination of women. Her entire life was a prayer; pain and suffering were accepted in that spirit, simply and without pretense.

During the years of my mother's illness, I continued to work at the center. We were both reading Merton. I was finding his writings on prayer and contemplation to be increasingly meaningful to me. My children were growing up.

With the end of the war, my attention shifted to the new strategies of counterforce coming out of the Nixon White House. The White House plumbers were getting all the publicity, as were detente and the opening of China. It wasn't yet known that Nixon's secret plan to end the war involved the threat to use the bomb. But the "humane" decision to target Soviet missile silos was awakening a few to a supposed "deterrence" policy which makes nuclear war much more likely.

The center began to organize an active campaign against the B-1 bomber. Its prime contractor, Rockwell International, was headquartered in Pittsburgh. We leafleted, demonstrated, lobbied, and finally decided to stage a sit-in in Rockwell's reception area on the 50th floor of the US Steel Building. Fourteen of us stayed for 25 hours before we were led away to an injunction hearing. We had a lot to learn about nonviolence, but the action generated publicity and was, we felt, "successful."

We later decided to challenge the B-1 bomber in court and spent time researching international law. I learned that these weapons of mass destruction were a violation of international treaties designed to limit the harm done to civilians. King and Gandhi had obeyed a higher law in their disobedience of unjust laws. Do not nuclear weapons result in injustice on a massive scale, involving the threat of extinction to all, including future generations?

Before our case could be heard, President Carter cancelled the B-1. The cruise missile would replace the B-1, creating an even more dangerous situation. Our "victory" turned to ashes.

I read *The Day Before Doomsday,* in which Sidney Lens outlined the developments in the arms race that were making nuclear war all but inevitable. Earlier I'd met and argued with Phil Berrigan, thinking his vision too harsh, but I was coming to see that his call for civil disobedience in the face of this kind of reality was really rather modest.

What might I have hoped to do to oppose Hitler's death camps had I lived at that time in Germany? The threat today is that the entire planet will become a death camp. As I pondered the fate of Franz Jagerstatter, a family man who refused to go along then, the threat of jail had to be weighed against the danger that my younger children might not live to grow up.

By the summer of 1979, when I was invited to participate in a retreat with Dan Berrigan on these questions, I summoned up my courage and went. I could evade no longer. As we reflected together on the Epistle of James, I realized that what was at stake was not only my life and that of my children, but my faith. If fear of the consequences were to prevent me from following the conclusions of my conscience, then what had I to give to my children that could measure up to my mother's gift to me? The transparency of her faith that shone throughout her life was precious inheritance.

After the retreat, I went home and prayed some more. I was ready to take a first step. In September I carried a photo of a child who had been injured by the bomb in Hiroshima and, with twenty others, I walked up the driveway of a Washington hotel where arms merchants had nuclear weapons on display at an "arms bazaar." Refused entry by the police, we knelt and prayed until we were arrested and charged with unlawful entry.

After agonizing for years, I felt a burden had been lifted. The experience of jail can be extremely dehumanizing, but for me it was an experience of freedom, freedom from the fears that had immobilized me and shackled my conscience.

As for jail, I prefer to think of it as an unpleasant task, such as cleaning the cellar, rather than a dramatic experience that is all too often an everyday reality for the very poor. The women I met in jail shared the little they had, looking out for the weakest among us. I had much to learn from them.

Once home, I continued to be involved in protests, including a nine-day fast for peace with a few friends. The experience deepened my own understanding of the centrality of prayer to all my actions. Soon afterwards, I learned of plans to attempt a direct act of disarmament against first-strike weapons. The consequences would be serious, perhaps years of separation from my family. Months of struggle followed. Was I trying to be a martyr? The complete relief I felt when told the project was off told me that a martyr complex was clearly not one of my characteristics. When plans resumed, I realized that, in Dan Berrigan's words, it was something that I could not *not* do.

Our passive acceptance of the bomb, which means our children's deaths, kills off our feelings. We shut out the reality, refusing to deal with it, experiencing a sort of death in life. In a terrible way we have already succumbed to the bomb, accepting it not only for ourselves, but for those we love. We narrow our sights and tacitly give up on the future, giving silent consent, then "forgetting."

More than anything, the generation growing up today, numbed by a world which offers them the bomb as inheritance, mesmerizing all of us into a sense of helplessness, needs the light of faith in a loving and powerful God, a God of hope who can stand in vulnerable counterforce to this idol of death. The past two years of jail, trial, appeals have not been without tension or continuing struggles within the family regarding ongoing resistance. I am deeply grateful for the words of my son, Gary, before I went to GE. Once he'd asked all the hard questions about my leaving his younger brothers, he said, "I guess you have to follow your conscience." In one way or another all of my children have come to that understanding. And, slowly, so have I.

Bill Kellermann

A Methodist Pastor

I want you to know, dear brothers and sisters, that what has happened to me has really served to advance the gospel, so that it became known throughout the whole praetorian guard and to all the rest that my imprisonment is for Christ; and most of the sisters and brothers have been made confident in the Lord because of my imprisonment, and are much more bold to speak the word of God without fear. (Philippians 1:12–14, RSV)

By the grace of God and the confirmation of my church, I am a Methodist pastor.

By that same providence (the givens of history and the leadings of the Spirit) I begin these reflections sitting at a hard metal table in tier F-2 of Richmond City Jail where several of us are confined a month for a simple symbolic witness at the Pentagon. The action with friends from Detroit was dramatic and liturgical and prayerful, an attempt to publicly confess and repent in ourselves and before all, the nuclear arms race.

From this table I have been trying clumsily to carry forward my pastoral responsibilities among the folk of a small congregation in Detroit. By correspondence I attempt little administrations, gather thoughts for a Bible study group, convey greetings to Sunday morning worshipers, and attend to some pastoral needs. This week a dear friend who has been languishing for many months died. So I suffer here the agony of separation and write to her husband a letter which cannot suffice (for either one of us) in place of being there.

I get pulled in a kind of tension.

It is put to me repeatedly from various quarters, left and

right, near and far, that there is a choice to be made: be a pastor or be a resister. The choice is tempting, an easy out. But given the gospel, given the bomb, given the calling of my heart, those two things (pastor and resister) seem to me inextricably one. Any forced choice, any "either/or" is falsely put. A violation of both, and finally of myself and my vocation.

I take up these reflections again, now many months later at the relative comfort of my desk at home. The intervening months, however, have not been so comfortable. Every attempt to return to this meditation has been frustrated or pre-empted by continuing crisis in my congregation concerning jailtime and debating whether the arms race bears in any way whatsoever on my pastoral duties. I have wished to resume writing in the same bold hope that informs Paul's letter to the Philippian community. But my experience, I confess, has been otherwise. My failings of heart and faith, my seeming failure in the congregation have made me doubt any authorization to speak. Nevertheless, by inspiration or bullheadedness, I remain steadfast in refusing false choices. I remain firmly convinced that nuclear resistance is pastoral business.

On my Pastor-Parish Relations Committee (where voices and opinions have been gracefully mixed) there is one member who utterly and forthrightly disagrees with me in substance over the arms race question. Strangely enough, he goes so far as to suggest that the bishop (who actively supports me) ought to grant me a full-time special appointment doing "peace work." The apparent contradiction is not just an easy get-him-out-of-my-pulpit solution; it is really an intuition and an insight. If "peace ministry" and resistance can be categorized and specialized and professionalized they will never truly connect with the life of a local congregation. They will never penetrate the church. Questions about the bomb can be kept political and thereby outside of worship, outside of faith, outside of that peculiar pastoral territory: the heart.

The fundamental problem, however, is that the bomb has already cast its shadow across our worship; it has launched a frontal assault on faith; it has invaded our hearts. The bomb is, and has been from the beginning, a pastoral concern.

In the Sermon on the Mount, Jesus makes clear that to imagine and intend a deed of violence is already to have done it in reality, in the heart, in the light of God's judgment. A warhead is armed and pointed at a city of human habitation. Where is the spiritual location of that intention? In the nether abstractions of computer program coordinates? In the mind of the powers? Or deeper, in the heart of a people? When the Hiroshima and Nagasaki bombs were set loose on the far side of the planet, they struck home in our hearts. When the MX or the cruise or the Trident are designed and built and targeted, they have already wreaked their devastation within us. Guilt, hardness of heart, despair, and spiritual confusion are the interior landscape (personal and communal) of that act and intention. They are cause and consequence of the arms race. And they are the field of the pastoral task.

We have, for example, entirely underestimated the dark burden of Hiroshima and the arms race guilt (I take them to be one and the same). That guilt functions politically in a very potent way precisely because it has been so little acknowledged. In the post-war years, as now, it was not seriously confronted, confessed, exposed, or otherwise ministered to.

Unacknowledged, unconfessed guilt strives with a hidden passion for self-justification. An early form of that justification was the yearning to believe that this terrifying new weapon held a secret good, a leap forward, a progress for all humanity. When "Atoms for Peace" was conceived it tapped that yearning to be justified in the bomb. The government's nuclear power program was not only a masterful cover for continued weapons development, but a brilliant stroke for the national psyche. It treated what the churches apparently failed to face. And we are still living (and slowly dying) with what has been called a "technological guilt trip": nuclear power.

It is not to minimize the economic powers, the military institutions, or the structures of ideology to say that guilt also drives the nuclear arms race forward. In the Hiroshima advent of atomic weapons there was a choice: We could either turn from them in horror, or justify them (their saving power to bring the boys home and end the war) by building more; choosing them yet again. To be "right" in choosing them then, we are compelled to choose them now again and again. Billions upon billions of dollars have been poured into the arms race; that is justified only if we carry it all absurdly forward. Guilt has a tenacious grip. There will be no letting go of these weapons, apart from confrontation with our own— personal and corporate—guilt.

To say amen to Hiroshima, to claim it as victory and embrace it was also to harden our hearts to the voices and sufferings of the victims. We could not look them in their burned and anguished faces and at the same time dance in the streets a victory celebration. Nor can we (please dear Lord) truly imagine the suffering and death of a nuclear blast and at the same time aim the missile, or even pay for it. Nuclear weapons harden our hearts. And not just to the nuclear victims.

Once we have accepted as a matter of policy a deliberate willingness to destroy entire cities—indeed, the planet (for whatever security or political motive)—how can we expect to take compassion on our neighbor next door or cross town? Contempt for the poor, for the aged, for our own cities is simply an extension of the contempt which the bomb holds for all humanity.

Hardened against the nuclear victim, hardened against our neighbor, we do well to remember that we become hardened against Christ, against, let us say, the Word of God. The parable of the sower might read something like this: A sower went out to sow and some of the seed fell on the hardened concrete of a missile silo. . . .

It is as though our hearts have been encased in (or worse, supplanted by) the super-hard concrete vault of a silo or a command post. Super-hardened hearts are the most indispensable feature of any nuclear weapons system—more a cornerstone than any single piece of technological hardware.

Nearly all the same things can be said of despair as well. Not long ago I was talking with some friends—a loose premarital counseling session in preparation for their marriage, in which I eventually shared. When pressed on the meaning of long-term commitment, one of them replied, "Well, with the bomb and all, never knowing when some big catastrophe will hit, it's hard to think about the long term and make those commitments." That knocked me over! These are not anti-nuclear activists counting down minutes on the doomsday clock of the *Atomic Scientists Bulletin,* or calculating the technological timeline for first-strike capability. These are just sensible and sensitive folks who live with a largely unspoken sense of doom: there is little or no future. And that sense affects their thinking about marriage commitments.

How much of the breakdown and breakup and break-apart we've all seen (trooping, for example through this pastor's study, not to mention his life and community) is related to the shadowy despair of the bomb?

More in the same vein: How much of our personal consuming,

our heavy credit buying, our devouring culture, our get-it-quick, use-it-all-now approach to economy and environment is based on despair of the future? Simply put in economic terms: You may as well buy it now and pay up later, because there may not be any later. A half-thought, smart-money wager. No one can measure, but it's not just speculation to suggest that our burning consumerism and mushrooming inflation is fueled in spirit by nuclear weaponry.

And, as with hardness of heart, this hidden, half-conscious despair functions politically on a massive scale. I believe that even more than fear, despair is the primary method of political control today. People resign themselves to inevitability, to the overwhelming momentum of the powers, before whom they feel so helpless. And they are thereby rendered passive spectators in their own history.

In the Book of Revelation, when the whole world follows after the Beast, they chant, "Who is like the Beast and who can fight against it?" Those are surely words of idolatrous awe and fear, of fascinated transfixion, but first and foremost they are words of despair. The whole world (save the faithful) falls into line and are led off captive by despair.

All of this traverses some landscape much too quickly. It is on the one hand political landscape which more deeply seen turns out to be interior, spiritual landscape. It covers just enough ground of the arms race to see that the heart of the matter is substantially a matter of the heart. A ministry and community which calls itself (or better, is called to be) pastoral must attend to the real causes and consequences of the bomb.

It will be no surprise to suggest that such a community might begin at its own center, at the heart of its life together: our Lord's Supper. In the simple mystery of the sacrament, grace has its means. There, in confession we are freed from guilt. There our hearts are renewed. There our hope embodied.

I am prone to complain that my church's conventional communion liturgy is overly penitential, relentless with heavy-handed breast beating. Still, confession is prerequisite to the meal. It is preparation and approach. It is laying out our broken lives and history up front and on the table, before one another and before the Lord. Communion is the singularly proper place to encounter and confess the nuclear arms race.

How can we ever forgive ourselves for the dropping of the

Hiroshima bomb? How can we forgive ourselves for launching and loosing Trident? How can we forgive ourselves for active tax paying complicity? How can we forgive ourselves the creeping sins of omission: our passive, idle silence? If we confess our sins, we can because we are forgiven in Christ—so say bread and wine. Now there is a pastoral word. I don't say lightly that we are forgiven Hiroshima. But I believe it, and I proclaim it as good news. The forgiveness of God (which not incidentally is near the center of any gospel nonviolence) is the only thing by which we are finally able to disentangle ourselves from the nuclear web. It is the freedom in which our own right action can arise. Apart from it, even good and solid nuclear resistance may be driven by guilt. That freedom and forgiveness is made concrete and accessible at the Lord's table.

Another way of saying this is that in Eucharist we are given a new heart. In the suffering death of Jesus, the body broken and the blood spilled, we come face to face with the suffering of the nuclear victims. Our hearts (God willing) get broken. Our super-hard concrete is pierced and crushed. What a grace it is when we can weep at the table of the Lord.

In that meal, in the new covenant in Christ's blood, an old promise is fulfilled: "And you shall be clean from all your uncleanness, and from all your idols I will cleanse you. A new heart I will give you, and a new spirit I will put within you; and I will take out of your flesh the heart of stone and give to you a heart of flesh" (Ezekiel 36). A healing in the deepest possible sense is effected.

Which is also to say again and again that the Eucharist is the sign of hope, in heart and in history. We eat the feast of promise "until the Lord comes." We live, even in the shadow of death, not resigned to death's final victory, but in daily anticipation of the kingdom, of the coming of judgment and grace, the vindication of truth, the sovereign rule of Christ. In communion, our hope of "what is and is to come" is nourished. Those who gather with bread and wine in their midst are precisely those who are not led off by despair and the nuclear beast.

Well, given the efficacious freedom of forgiveness and renewed hearts and embodied hope, you would think that congregations breaking communion bread day after day would be hotbeds of nuclear resistance. Needless to say, that has not heretofore been so. The Lord's Supper has in fact been subjected in our time to a great spiritual confusion. It has been betrayed and diluted and compromised. (Here we come closest to the matter of pastoral negligence.)

I hear it said, directly and indirectly, that our freedom to celebrate the Lord's Supper is won and secured, granted and guaranteed by our nuclear arsenal! I have this picture of the altar ringed with missiles pointing outward, guarding and protecting the elements of freedom. The vision is extreme but not, I think, unfair to what is being proclaimed even from some pulpits.

That "freedom" proffered by the powers, and the freedom, even to die, proclaimed and offered by Christ at table—are two categorically different things. And yet they have been confused, and mingled, and mistaken.

When Paul writes to the community at Corinth, the very letter in which he delivers again to them that which he received from the Lord, the words of eucharistic institution (our earliest record of the communion prayer), he precedes all that with a great warning (1 Corinthians 10):

> Therefore, my brothers and sisters, shun the worship of idols. I speak as to sensible people; judge for yourselves what I say. The cup of blessing which we bless, is it not a participation in the blood of Christ? The bread which we break, is it not a participation in the body of Christ? . . . What do I imply then? That food offered to idols is anything, or that an idol is anything? No, I imply that what pagans sacrifice they offer to demons and not go God. I do not want you to be partners with demons. You cannot drink the cup of the Lord and the cup of demons. You cannot partake of the table of the Lord and the table of demons.

Yes, of course, communion is a gift. Its healing forgiveness and renewal and hope are a grace that we receive with empty and open hands. But it is also a *choice:* between Christ and the idols, between God and the gods of this world. American Christians, especially, have tried to have it both ways, barely noticing the missile come close and come between at the altar. I submit that this is why the healing and freeing power of the Eucharist has been minimized and muted. The pastoral task, the sacramental task, is to make that choice simple and utterly clear.

Pastors and pastoral communities will make the choice clear at the altar with bread in hand and whispered intercession. But they will also need to make it clear, let us say, "in the streets." It remains a twofold mystery that this most interior, contemplative act of choice and grace in the community is a "political" threat to the rule of the powers (that is partly the implication of all that goes before) and, at the same time, that the public, dramatic acts of confrontation that well might be called "political" are among the most pastoral ministrations to the heart.

This is most clearly the case with our Pastor, Christ. He attends to the deepest needs of our hearts by his bold actions in the streets of Jerusalem. In his arrest and trial and execution on the cross, Jesus is being our pastor. It is, in fact, that public drama which the Last Supper contemplates. It points to and remembers and rehearses exactly those events.

When Jesus speaks openly about pastoring in John 10, he doesn't invoke an idyll of lambs gamboling quietly in summer pastures. The Good Shepherd passage is a straightforward warning about deceivers and confusers and misleaders, about thieves who come to "kill and destroy." It is about not heading the other direction when the devouring beast appears on the prowl. It is, let us be utterly clear, about risk and action. The Shepherd and Pastor lays down freely his life.

I will be the first to confess my weakness and fear before such a call and claim. But I come back to it. I believe it has everything to do with how Paul is able to write of pastoral encouragement from jail to the congregation at Philippi. It certainly authorizes some hope for going to the Pentagon or GE or Lockheed or an arms bazaar or such like, with an intercession for history and heart. And I'm thoroughly convinced that it requires us in community and ministry to explore active resistance as a pastoral tactic and concern.

Mary Lou Kownacki

A Member of a Religious Community

In a Xerox ad on TV, a short, fat monk performs the "miracle" of finding a duplicating machine to copy in record time all the materials requested by his abbot. I find the ad a fitting parable on the state of much of contemporary monasticism in this country.

The image of monasticism is still embedded in a false romanticism, characterized in the ad by strains of Gregorian chant, pealing bells, long robes, and work by candlelight. The romantic is kept in balance, of course, by pointing out that monks have indeed adapted to the modern age. Like the majority of Americans, monastics have greeted with open arms all that technology has to offer, blessing it as good—Xerox machines rather than hand-crafted letters being just one example. But the worst indictment is saved for the end—we all smile at the pudgy little monk who gazes pie-eyed towards the heavens and say, "Isn't he cute." I see all of America patting monastery after monastery, convent after convent on the head and saying, "Aren't they nice." No need to take monasticism seriously; it threatens no person or institution.

Monastic orders are especially notorious for promoting the idea that sanctity depends on separation from the world, on being different from other human beings. Pictures of hooded figures strolling through the woods and gazing at streams probably have helped sell countless books and records, but they have also reinforced the idea that holiness and peace are found by fleeing the evil world. Bishop Thomas Gumbleton struck home when he said: "It's too easy for monks to be apart from the world and therefore untouched by the world and consequently unable to touch the world either."

The irony is that while monastics have tried to project a "beyond the world" spirituality, they have been as eager as the rest of the world to grasp and accumulate all that the American dream has to offer. What started out as a counterculture revolution now mirrors the society to a grotesque degree. We've bought it all: bigger is better and so is "more"; the United States is the light of the world; any technological innovation is "progress"; capitalism is next to godliness. And, yes, nuclear weapons make sure that God stays on our side.

Monastics aren't blatant about these things; like the rest of middle-class America, they just fit in. That's the horror. Who these days would equate monasticism with a resistance movement? But that's what it once was.

Anthony, Martin of Tours, Benedict of Nursia, and other great monastic figures stood as question marks to the values of their culture. Their positions on the linkage of church and state, injustice, oppression of the poor, accumulation of wealth, and violence may not have been popular, but at least their lives were taken seriously. Now people visit the monasteries to "get away from it all," to buy cheese and holy cards, to hear nice singing, and to sell Xerox machines.

I'm not being completely fair. Monasteries do serve as an oasis for people, constant reminders that silence, solitude, and prayer are essential for peace of heart and effective ministry. It's also true that monastic communities, like all religious orders, are attempting to renew, to rediscover the spirit of the founder and come to grips with what it means to preach Jesus today. Documents dealing with contemporary spirituality, simple lifestyle, social justice, and world peace are pouring out of religious houses. Certainly, all the position papers have borne some fruit. However, it's mainly the lives of individual religious or small pockets within the larger community that have been transformed. Most institutions still taste neither hot nor cold, tempting Jesus to vomit them out of his mouth.

"Here it goes again," I can hear people say. "Another strident article filling religious with guilt because they are not in destitution or in jail or setting up campsites on the front lawn of the Pentagon." Not really. There are other possibilities.

Let's imagine a scenario in which a community has made a corporate commitment to nuclear disarmament; that is, the entire community has agreed to promote this issue no matter where they are or in how many diverse ministries they might be engaged. Let me tell you how it works; let me tell you how it might.

The process I will describe is not only a model that other

religious orders may follow, but gives an example of how parishes, congregations, and base communities can confront the nuclear issue.

My community, the Benedictine Sisters of Erie, has taken nuclear disarmament as its corporate commitment. It is an issue that we feel touches the core of the monastic charism, not just of peace but of community building. After all, the whole concept of nuclear disarmament is a community-building act; nuclear arms are community destroying.

We fleshed out this commitment in ways as diverse as are the members and expressions of peacemaking throughout monastic history. First, a press release was issued to national and local media which stated: "... the Benedictine Sisters of Erie will stand in a corporate way for the nuclear disarmament of the nations in behalf of the value of created life ... each of us individually will stand for that purpose in whatever way we can wherever we are."

But church groups are notorious for issuing strong peace and justice statements; their records are less impressive when it comes to actions. The Erie Benedictines did not want to fall into the trap of hollow words. Immediately after adopting the corporate ministry the community council voted to send $100 a month to Pax Christi USA and 10 percent of all income from community fund raisers. Although the financial contribution was minimal, it was an expression of sustenance sharing. The 140 member community is half-a-million dollars in debt, and every extra cent earned goes toward the debt. Also, to a fledgling organization like Pax Christi, it was a boon.

To keep the issue before the public eye, articles on nuclear disarmament and community actions are included in the Benedictine's quarterly newsletter, which goes to 10,000 friends, benefactors, and family members. The community also sponsors workshops on this issue and hosts an annual peace liturgy for the general public. More than 1,500 people gathered on the front lawn of Mount Saint Benedict in the summer of 1980 to join the monks of Western Priory and the Benedictine Sisters of Erie in a joyful celebration for world peace. Before the liturgy began, a world flag was raised on the flagpole in front of the Erie Priory. It continues to fly above the U.S. flag, a symbol that for the Erie Benedictines world community takes precedence over narrow national interests.

Our community owns only one educational institution, a high

school for girls. Since this institution is an extension of the Benedictine community, the corporate commitment to nuclear disarmament is a top priority there. In addition to a strong peace and justice curriculum, the school has taken the added step of not permitting military recruiters or any of their materials into the school.

Needless to say, this strong antiwar stance, along with a high profile on the women's issue, has met with some public resistance. At one lay board meeting, for example, when an increase in tuition was being discussed along with an explanation of why enrollment had dropped, one of the board members said, "Well, you can't expect parents to dish out $700 a year to send a girl to St. Ben's so that you can teach them to demonstrate." The principal informed him that social justice and peace were integral to the school's philosophy and would be taught, even if it meant a drop in enrollment.

Sr. Joan Chittister, prioress of the community, takes every opportunity to call attention to the peace issue. When the Erie Benedictines drew national attention for striking natural gas on their property, Chittister was interviewed in *People* magazine and injected the following:

> People ask us constantly if we think this was a miracle. We don't. We have a commitment here to raising consciousness about world peace, conservation and the dangers of nuclear weaponry. To us, a miracle will be when we can all develop a sense of responsibility toward each other and for the world we live in.

Although the symbolic and communal responses are strategic, what's happening to individual members is more revolutionary in terms of long-range effects. At the annual "blessing of ministries" ceremony, each sister must indicate on paper what she, as an individual, will do to carry out the corporate commitment. The opening paragraph of the ministry statement reads:

> Basic to the ministry of our community this year is nuclear disarmament. I will support this corporate ministry, and other areas of peace and justice, in the following ways . . ."

The responses, which are presented to the prioress, are as multiple as members of the community:

- Veronica sponsors a peace fair at the grade school where she is principal;
- Ann has joined Pax Christi and sends $2 a month out of her personal budget;
- Marlene is helping to organize a national group called Benedictines for Peace;
- Annette has promised to write one letter a month to a friend or family member on the nuclear issue;
- Rosanne is joining a public fast during Lent as a sign of repentance for complicity in the nuclear arms race;
- Kathleen has designed a reading course for herself on the Church's teachings on war.

In addition, social justice and peace are integral to the liturgical life of the community and there is ongoing education on disarmament. During two consecutive Lenten seasons, for example, the community has done special readings on peace and disarmament.

One of the first questions asked about the corporate commitment is: "How did you get everyone to back a single issue, especially one that controversial?"

The Erie Benedictines have a simple answer: We didn't wait for everyone to agree on the issue. What the community did agree on was that it wanted a corporate commitment. By straw vote the community indicated that it was interested in three issues: world hunger, women, nuclear disarmament. Workshops were presented to all community members on each topic and a vote was taken to determine which one would be adopted. Because the issues before us were massive, important, and frankly, remote from us at that point in history (1978), the consensus of the community was that we would back any of the three that a majority of us wanted. We had already agreed unanimously that these were difficult issues to choose among and that we would go with the insights and the readiness of the greater number of people.

"I don't think there is another way to go at this corporate commitment," Chittister explained. "You have to start someplace. And you don't start with everybody sure and everybody comfortable. You start most things with trust. That's the essence of consensus and that's what I think the community gave."

After having been in it a year, after having faced brothers who had fought in Korea and nephews who returned from Vietnam, after being the butt of countless "naive nun" remarks, the Erie

Benedictines were given the opportunity at a community meeting to withdraw from the idea of a corporate commitment altogether or to choose another or to stay with nuclear disarmament. By a 90 percent consensus, they voted on a three-year commitment to nuclear disarmament.

"The corporate commitment has brought a kind of 'spirituality of the anawim' that we haven't felt in a long time and maybe hadn't had in our lifetime," explained Chittister. "It's touched our liturgy, our hospitality, our use of resources, our individual conversations—people begin to see what it is to be counterculture, not just functional. Previously we told ourselves that somehow or another a gospel life was a different life, and we marked ourselves off as different in a million ways—we lived behind walls, we wore uniforms, we had a highly structured lifestyle that was not the family lifestyle in the culture. Then we came to realize that those differences weren't necessarily gospel differences, but cultural differences. Now our stance on nuclear disarmament is bringing us to the heart of what it is to hold a value in the gospel that is neither convenient, pragmatic, capitalistic, or comfortable for a lot of people. It touches spirituality, I think, at its core."

The most important aspect of the corporate commitment, therefore, is its call to personal conversion. The Erie Benedictines have called themselves to conversion. If others also hear the call, that's an extra.

So far so good. But greater risks need to be taken in this area, I think, and whether or not the Erie Benedictines or any other monastic group will chance these remains to be seen.

For example, what effect would it have if the oldest religious community in the Catholic Church proclaimed publicly that nonviolence was an essential monastic value? What would it mean if those entering Christian monastic communities were required to take a vow of nonviolence?

When I asked Bede Griffith, the Benedictine monk who lives in an ashram in India, what he thought about this idea, he wrote:

I think a nonviolent attitude to life as expressed in the Sermon on the Mount should be basic to monastic life and could very well be the subject of a vow. It would apply to one's attitude to nature, rejecting all violation of nature by science and technology, showing a loving concern for plants and animals as well as for men and opposing the violence of political and economic structure. As I suggested in *Christ in India,* ahimsa (nonviolence) should be integral to monastic life, extending not only to rejection of war and heavy armaments but also to heavy industry and nuclear power, seeking to create a society of peace with nature and with God.

The whole issue of religious paying war taxes will soon be a major problem. Tax exemption no longer holds for religious who work outside community institutions. Individual members can refuse to pay the percentage of federal income tax that feeds the war machine—and take the consequences. But a communal commitment to war tax resistance could also be expressed by establishing a special community fund where individual religious as well as laity could send their war tax money to be used for programs that meet basic human needs. This would put the community as well as individual members in jeopardy.

I also look forward to the day when convents and monasteries reclaim their ancient role as sanctuaries, safe places for those fleeing from the law. Our homes could harbor "criminals" who nonviolently break laws to protect life. Those who commit civil disobedience to protest the nuclear arms race, all nuclear pacifists who refuse to serve in the armed forces if the draft is reinstated should find refuge in our homes and every effort made to explain their position to the wider public, every risk taken to protect them.

There are deeper, more fundamental questions that need to be addressed: lifestyle and the sacred cows of capitalism and nationalism. Tom Cullinan, a Benedictine monk who founded an experimental community outside of Liverpool, England, and who has written extensively on peace and justice has noted: "Too many groups work at the level of nuclear arms or arms sales and not enough ask why it is that wealthy nations need armaments. There's a tie-in between the arms race and our concept of ownership, what it means for a thing to be mine or yours. If I've got things, I have to defend them; if I own things I have to lock my front door. And it's at this deep level that monastic life ought to be relevant. We ought to say that nothing ever belongs to any of us. We need a new vision of ownership. But we can only say it by doing it, not by merely voicing it."

Yes, we do need more than symbolic actions. We need the

peace curriculums, the petitions, the lobbying, the political analysis, the religious statements on peace, the books and articles on nuclear disarmament. But we are desperate for something more. I think we all begin by trying to put new wine into old wineskins; my hope is that we don't stop when the wine begins to seep through the cracks, the tears.

Vincent Harding

A Black Historian

In the fall of 1953, when I began my sojourn there, Fort Dix, New Jersey, did not advertise itself as a place of awakening. Rather, in the ominous interregnum between the quieting of the war in Korea and the heating of the U.S. war in Vietnam, that sprawling army base served as a major reception center and training ground for tens of thousands of this country's draftees. I was among them, arriving at Dix late in the summer, coming out of Harlem and the South Bronx shortly after my twenty-second birthday.

As I approached this new experience (aside from three summers of work at camps, I had never been away from home ground for an extended period), I brought with me a mixed and sometimes tortured array of feelings. On the one hand, I had been deeply nourished by a church fellowship that encouraged its drafted young men to apply for non-combatant status—such as the Medical Corps. On the other hand, I had decided that I would move right into the infantry for several reasons. One was that I wanted to be opened to the mainstream military experience that was marking the lives of so many of my generation.

Second, I was filled with wanderlust, and considered the army a marvelous opportunity to see the world—especially since the United States now appeared to be no longer engaged in active warfare anywhere. Besides, for many strange reasons that cannot be developed here, I thought I wanted to be an officer, and sixteen weeks of infantry basic training was the first requirement for anyone who chose to explore that option. (It turned out, by the way, that neither my second nor my third ambition was fulfilled—how marvelous the ways of grace that shut doors in your face! But the first, infantry training, was sufficiently arranged to provide the basis for my awakening.)

It was in the course of that experience with "basic" that I

repeatedly found myself stretched out flat on my belly, handling first a rifle, then a machine gun, learning to become reasonably accurate at hitting targets up to 500 yards away. I would not have chosen the penetrating cold of Fort Dix's early winter, or its chilling sandy soil, as the situation best suited to an awakening, but that is what began to happen.

For a time I was enjoying the firing range, thinking of what I was doing as a kind of sport, appreciating the power of the sun when it finally came out to warm us in those early mornings. Then—I'm not sure when or how—it occurred to me that the army was not expending money and ammunition to teach me some enjoyable sport; instead, what was really happening was that I was learning how to kill another human being without ever having to see his or her face.

The message began to seep in, penetrating like the winds that so often swept across the range. I was being forced to deal with issues that I had avoided, questions that had been pushed aside. Then, not long after, it all broke out into the open as we engaged in bayonet drill: for there was no way that I could mistake this for sport. Here, the drill sergeant—following the traditions of bayonet training—was urging us to scream and roar and snarl like animals, as we learned how to maneuver ourselves and our deadly weapon into position to tear out the guts of another person.

Sometimes they said that the terrible sounds were meant to throw the opponent off guard, but we knew that something terrible was at work. We were being pressed toward an alternate identity, urged to become something wild and savage, something less than human, something that impelled us to deny our fundamental identity as children of the loving God, something that would make it possible for us to cut out the life of our brother, our sister, with one well-trained stroke, and then to accept the justifying prayers and sermons of those who were paid to bless our work.

Several of us were deeply disturbed by what we were doing, frightened at times by the army's campaign against our humanity, perhaps even more frightened by the capacities we saw within ourselves to cooperate, at least to submit. But we weren't sure what to do, or perhaps we were sure that we didn't have the courage to do what was necessary—quit, resign, refuse to cooperate. (The models for that were not widespread in 1953 and 1954.)

As a child of the church, I went to the chaplains. I needed

help in knowing what my riflery and bayonet skills had to do with the love of Christ for all people, with the teachings I had received at Victory Tabernacle in Harlem. I asked the military pastors how they—and I—might put together in one life the mission of the army to seek out the enemy and destroy them and the mission of the church, the mission of God's children, to be channels of love and service. I asked, sometimes with tears welling up, how could I, with bayonet in hand, be a follower of him who threw open his arms to his enemies?

But the chaplains could not (would not?) help me. One who was black and a captain simply said that each of us had to work out such conflicts for ourselves. He had dealt with his conflicts—not without occasional questions, he admitted—and I must deal with mine, essentially alone. Obviously, the army did not pay its pastors to counsel people out of the military.

If I had had courage and wisdom enough, I would have worked my own way toward a dishonorable discharge then, would have refused to continue service on such compromised terms. Instead, for the rest of my two years, I stayed and worked my way out within the army, distanced myself as far as possible from its apparatus of death, created my own living space, vowed forever to oppose the way of the bayonet and seek the way of the open arms.

That was the beginning for me. My search for a humanity-building alternative to nuclear war began at Fort Dix, that training ground for the waging of "conventional" war, began when I was forced to recognize the fundamental contradiction between the bayonet and the cross. Of course, I could not know how much was opening then, but no matter; how often do we recognize new beginnings when they come?

And yet I did know some things. I knew I wanted to find a way of life consistent with the commitments I had made in the military. (At least I wanted it in theory, but only partly in practice; for I have long since discovered that at the deepest levels of practice I had and have a long way to go.) So when I left Fort Dix in 1955 and shortly thereafter found my way to Chicago, I was on a pilgrimage: a hybrid academic, moving between the university's graduate history department and its theological faculties, serving as part-time lay minister for a small, black southside congregation. I was in search.

It was at the university that I first discovered the life and witness of the sixteenth-century Anabaptist communities and their often radical commitment to the Christ of the open arms. They appealed to me. Their discipline, self-sacrificing love, defying the powers of kings and rulers who tried to turn them from the demands of their Master, their willingness to accept death rather than inflict suffering—these things seemed somehow directly related to the awakening at Fort Dix.

So I was open to their twentieth-century descendants when they came to me from Woodlawn Mennonite Church on Chicago's southside and asked if I would help in a team ministry that sought to apply the ways of peace to the racial conflicts of our time. Maintaining my status as a lay person, I joined the team in 1958. As I moved into the world of the peace churches, the pacifist movement and the teachers of nonviolent resistance to injustice, I came to Gandhi again. (Long ago, at Victory Tabernacle Church in Harlem, I remembered my pastor speaking proudly to us of Garvey and others, as well as of Gandhi, "that little brown man who has turned the British Empire upside down.") Since then, he has remained a consistent presence, a teacher whose depths I have only begun to explore.

In the peace church context, I came, too, to Rosemarie Freeney of Georgia and Chicago. She had been part of the Mennonite setting before me, had begun to explore the connections between the traditions of blackness and the traditions of peacemaking. Of course, at that very moment the issue was being joined with great energy and creativity in the South, and we were married in the year that the black student movement began to awaken the nation. In that same year, 1960, we went to one of the local churches and heard some of the southern student movement participants as they told their stories and sang their songs from the frontlines. We had already experienced Martin Luther King, Jr., in a Chicago lecture, and I had met him in Montgomery.

Somehow, we could not escape the calling of these voices and these lives. Here, on our own soil, mounting numbers of men and women who were bone of our bone and flesh of our flesh were carrying on one of humankind's most crucial struggles. Not only were they defying the old order in search of racial justice and citizenship rights (that would be grand in itself), but some of them were bold enough, visionary enough, to speak of "redeeming the soul of America," daring to see the power of nonviolence as a force for the transformation of the entire American nation.

For me, there was something that connected those southern campaigns with my own struggles of the soul at Fort Dix, with my own fledgling commitment to a world of peace and freedom, a society of justice and truth. For in the face of bayonets and their equivalent, these black men and women, with their songs of faith and courage, with their white allies in hope, had chosen to experiment with tough, disciplined, self-sacrificing love. Their call from the South seemed to be a call to us, so Rosemarie and I found ourselves in Atlanta before the end of 1961.

We were sponsored by the international service committee of the Mennonite churches, and one of our first tasks was to establish Mennonite House in Atlanta. Without model or precedent, it became a combination residence for an interracial team of local movement participants and social service volunteers, a house of refuge for field workers from the various movement organizations, an ecumenical community, and a base of operations for our own ministry of reconciliation.

It was from that base that we moved out to participate in freedom struggle activities throughout the South, but it was also from here that we engaged in our first antinuclear war demonstration. For several days in October 1962, at the height of the U.S.–USSR impasse over Cuban missile installations, as John Kennedy threatened the use of nuclear weapons, some of us from Mennonite House joined other movement-oriented Atlantans—and concerned citizens across the country—in a daily vigil of protest and hope.

During those perilous days, as we stood in a park area near the heart of the city, there was no division in our hearts. This action on behalf of humankind, this urgent calling of men away from their nuclear bayonets, seemed totally at one with the work we were doing in places like Albany, Georgia, Selma, Alabama, and Greenwood, Mississippi. Together, this black and white company of witnesses was proclaiming that the struggle was undivided. (Indeed, we were assured of that when some of the same detectives and FBI men we had known from our movement activities also appeared at the antinuclear peace vigil, some taking names, others attempting to intimidate, refusing to loose their holds on the old ways of life and death.) Part of our struggle, we were saying, was for freedom from the fear of nuclear annihilation. Part of our struggle, we declared, was to work for so fundamental a way of justice that the sources of enmity would eventually be withdrawn from our nation's dealings with Cuba and Russia and all others defined as "enemy."

Mennonite House was itself a gathering place for the forces of that multifaceted community of struggle. Indeed, all of the movement's tendencies sooner or later found their way there, from local Islamic leaders to the dedicated southern white students who were trying to find a place of service for themselves in the van of history.

Our daughter, Rachel Sojourner, was born into that peripatetic household of struggle and hope, and the quest for world peace and for justice and community in our sector of the world is joined in her. She was with us as we marched in Birmingham. She was in her stroller as we picketed Hubert Humphrey for his contribution to the mounting war in Vietnam. She was visibly present within Rosemarie as we stood out under the sky in Atlanta, refusing to hide from any missiles, knowing that our calling was to throw open our arms, seeking to draw forth the powers of peace on behalf of the unborn. She carries Fort Dix and Birmingham in her bones. She is a witness to the oneness of the vision.

Nevertheless, in all of this, we were constantly aware of our own deepening need for peace, for unity, for re-creation, and our family left Atlanta near the end of 1964 in search of renewal. It was of great importance that we spent our time in the midst of a Christian communitarian fellowship whose members were committed to the ways of peacemaking on personal, national, and international levels.

When we returned to Atlanta late in the spring of 1965, I had finally finished my doctorate (which had been left undone when we went south in 1961) and was scheduled to chair the department of history and sociology at Spelman College beginning that fall. But first, something had to be dealt with. For reasons that I did not fully understand, the mounting American warfare against the Vietnamese had been tearing at me. I knew very little about the history of that conflict, but I had certain suspicions about U.S. intentions among the nonwhite and I determined to learn as much as I could. So, on Hiroshima Day, 1965, I set aside all other preparations for teaching and committed myself to dig into the documents on the war until I could sense for myself what was going on.

What I learned was deeply disturbing, and I began to speak and write as widely as I could about what seemed to me the fundamental injustice involved in America's role in that situation, from our government's support of the French colonialists in the years right after World War II, to the terrifying and destructive situation that was then building as American troops poured onto the anguished peninsula. Again, because I saw no separation between my engagement in the black struggle for freedom and new humanity in the U.S. and the movement for peace and justice and human liberation across the globe, one of my first concerns was to communicate my own convictions to some of my comrades in the freedom movement. A letter, sent to the 1965 Southern Christian Leadership Conference (SCLC) convention in Birmingham, Alabama was the result. It called for a prophetic word of judgment to be spoken concerning the nation's policies in Vietnam.

Certainly, my voice was not unique in the movement. The radicalized young people of the Student Non-Violent Coordinating Committee had already proclaimed their uncompromising opposition to the war and the draft. Malcolm X had seen and spoken the truth of the situation before his death. Home folks in the black communities of Mississippi had begun to receive the boxes with the bodies of their sons, and they were raising the inevitable questions about the fight for Vietnamese freedom that our government was supposedly waging, when so much unfinished freedom business still remained in every single county of their state.

Of course, the unfinished business of America—the nation's rampant racism, its continued exploitation of its own non-white peoples—was not confined to the South. Soon all its shame was exposed for the world to see as the flames of rebellion sprang from northern streets and northern hearts to reveal a racial scar extending across the length of the continent, from Harlem to Watts, and in many unexpected places along the way.

From within the life of the black movement, we saw these things as wide-ranging plebiscites of fire against the war in Vietnam. We translated the burning buildings and raging hearts into so many votes against the tremendous human waste involved in devoting so much money to the building of life-threatening nuclear arsenals. And there was no mistaking the new energy that was coming into the antiwar movement in the mid-sixties as people like Bob Moses, Stokeley Carmichael, Jim Bevel, Fannie Lou Hamer, and Martin Luther King, Jr., began to enter the fray.

The rise of the black power movement in the late 1960s

brought another powerful element from the black community back into the struggle for a new, unthreatening world order. When Stokeley and others yelled, "Hell No, We Won't Go," they were witnessing to more than black opposition to the war, or refusal of the draft. Deeper still was a generations-old tradition of trenchant black criticism of American foreign policy, especially in relationship to nonwhite peoples.

So when I heard the protestors, I heard Paul Robeson and W. E. B. DuBois more than a decade earlier, sharply criticizing America's reactionary stand at the side of its colonialist allies, against the liberation struggles of the nonwhite world. Hearing them I heard again the black socialist at the end of the nineteenth century, watching his people being drawn into support for the American ventures in Cuba and the Philippines, saying, "The American Negro cannot become the ally of Imperialism without enslaving his own race."

And I thought of the black soldiers in that Spanish-Cuban-American war embarking from Florida to fight in Cuba, stuffed into the bottom decks of the ships (perhaps remembering an earlier ocean crossing by their foreparents, also below decks), while their white counterparts enjoyed the run of the upper levels.

And I remembered the black soldiers going off in 1917 and 1918 to "make the world safe for democracy," while the screams of massacred black men, women, and children rang out from places like East St. Louis, Illinois. And I was buried with the rebellious black soldiers in Houston, Texas, who finally rose up in 1917 against the brutality of the white community, and found themselves secretly courtmartialed, secretly executed, and secretly interred, with army vehicles running over their burial place, as the authorities sought to ensure that the contagion of their commitment to freedom would not be set loose among the war-bond buying, Europe-marching black community. Nor could I forget those who came home from World War II to be lynched with their uniforms still on. (Sometimes it is hard to be a historian of the black experience in this land. The dreams and memories are powerful to bear.)

Indeed, all this reminded me that Langston Hughes spoke for the deepest part of us all when he wrote "America, you've never been America to me." And from the most honest levels of our lives we could almost have supplied him another line or two for foreign

e of the men and women from their
t days in the 1960s. Now, my essen-
, for them, and other black people to
en our role in the humanizing of the
the importance of the continuing chal-

I suggested that we now need openly,
rces that are poisoning and destroying
h, that we must take on the larger ques-
all peoples are unemployed, that we are
of those who stand against the militarism
ce that threatens humankind with nuclear
ng how much engagement we were able to
ting, and one of the constant themes raised
"black folks don't have time to deal with
nuclear threat or world economy now; we're
o survive."

d them that from our earliest days on these
rvival was a very precarious matter, we have
selves to more than physical survival. We have
n's concept of freedom, we have created songs
ental issues of ethics and spirituality, we have
ibilities for black and white co-habitation and
 nation—all the while living with our backs

d in the lounge in Jackson, and believe deeply
at a challenge like the fate of the earth is ours to
the past, we black folk have never been too desper-
. Now our future depends upon our willingness to
eat humanizing tradition of our foreparents, joining
ho share a common vision of a new humanity, ac-
nd participating in the leadership of the hard, long
ew American reality. That is the ultimate context of
ght against nuclear destruction. Essentially, it is a
other Earth, for the honor of our foreparents, for the
ildren. To opt out of that struggle is to opt out of life.
r been too desperate to be human.
nk you, Martin. Thank you, Malcolm. Thank you, Du-
obeson. Thank you, Ella Baker. Thank you, Medgar
Rosa Parks. Thank you, Ida B. Wells and Reverdy Ran-

policy: "So don't go around fighting no wars in my name, America, and don't send me no invitations if you do."

Seeing life from the bottom up, watching developments from the black side, perhaps we saw something that too many others missed. Surely DuBois and Robeson had seen it: On one level the American nuclear arsenal was simply another set of weapons being used by the nation to push forward a foreign policy that was essentially flawed and corrupted by its racist, anticommunist, and antiliberationist commitments. Indeed, it may be that our nonwhite experience in the United States continually forced us to a key insight: There can be no significant future for an antinuclear weapons movement that does not face up to the fundamental injustice in the nation's dealings with the poor and nonwhite world. From the perspective of our experiences, that set of relationships is at least as important as the more publicized standoff with the Soviet Union. At least that is how it appeared to me as I delved into our history and moved toward our future.

In a way, all of this came to a head in Martin Luther King, Jr. Here was the best known spokesperson for the black freedom movement in the United States, a man also fully identified with the search for nonviolent solutions to international conflict, and an early opponent of nuclear weaponry. After having been awarded a Nobel Prize for Peace in 1964 (and receiving it on behalf of the black freedom movement), he felt a more urgent need than ever before to fulfill his role as spokesman for world peace, especially on behalf of the poor. As he expanded his vocal opposition to the war, indicating the toll he saw it exacting at home and abroad, King was aware of the fact that he was placing himself in direct opposition to Lyndon Johnson. Because the president's support of the black community's struggles for justice was considered essential, and because it was well known that Johnson's angry reaction to opposition could be dangerous, many persons in the civil rights establishment sought to deter King from his path. By the fall of 1966, Johnson himself made a major move to try to dissuade Martin.

Counting on the supposedly impeccable liberal credentials of his ambassador to the United Nations, Arthur Goldberg, the president proposed that King meet privately with Goldberg for a briefing on U.S. foreign policy in general and on Vietnam in particular. As part of the preparation for that encounter, Andy Young (who surely never realized that he would one day be in Goldberg's role) spoke to me. Recalling my earlier call for solidarity with the Vietnamese people, he asked me to prepare a document for Martin, outlining the history of the Indochinese revolutionary struggle, focusing on the American involvement in the situation, suggesting some steps that might be taken from a liberationist perspective.

As we know, the conversation with Goldberg did nothing to turn Martin from his principaled opposition to the war. Instead, he stepped up his pace, and before long Andy Young and I were conferring again, this time about the possibility of my preparing a draft document that could serve as the basis for a major statement on Vietnam by Martin. Eventually that document became the core of King's Riverside Church speech in April 1967.

Because I believe that there is a direct, relational line between Martin's stand at Riverside that evening and his death in the night exactly one year later in Memphis, I have at times had mixed feelings about my own role in the creation of that statement. Sometimes I've asked if I helped to expose him to the forces who arranged for his death. Did my ideas and convictions press him beyond his own, toward the sights of the gun? Most often, my response—and that of those close to me—has been that I must give Martin space to be his own man. He would not have spoken the words as his own if he had not made them his own. In proclaiming them to the world, he took full responsibility for the dangers he knew they entailed. Besides, he was no stranger to such risks; he had been consciously, courageously living with them for a long time.

In the speech, we tried to make clear that there was much more at stake for our nation than the ending of the war in Vietnam. We tried again to come from the underside, to see America and the world through the eyes of those who had been broken and humiliated by the arrogant power of the white West. From this perspective, there seemed no true opening to a humane future in our land save the path of revolutionary transformation in America. Martin knew that it was entirely possible for the war in Vietnam to end without America's basic direction being changed. And he would certainly know now that significant nuclear disarmament might take place with his country still "on the wrong side of the world's revolutions"; still using its highly technologized "conventional forces" against the aspirations of the peoples of the nonwhite world.

som. Thank you, Angelo Herndon and Langston Hughes. Thank you, all of you, and those who birthed you, who were never too desperate to be human.

We join hands with you, A. J. Muste and Clarence Jordan. We walk together, Bob Spike and Tom Merton. You cannot escape our embrace, Anne Braden, Will Campbell, and Dorothy Day. Thank you, all of you. And thank you, Victory Tabernacle. And you, Fort Dix, cold, disguised, windswept awakening ground. Thank you.

We are awakening to our calling. God of the universe, God of the open arms, thank you. We are awakening. We, the people. We are awakening.

Richard Barnet

A Policy Analyst

I was sixteen when the bomb went off. Amid exultation at the technical marvels of nuclear annihilation, the early commentators struck a persistent note of fear, and this made an indelible impression on me. Though America had an exclusive hold on the "secret" of the bomb, no one was safe. Someone else could make the bomb, and the nuclear "trustee," as Truman called us, was no longer defendable. I was not good at high school physics, but I was good enough to understand that there was no longer a secret. Destruction on such a scale had burst the bonds of nationality, and the bomb would be no respector of borders. Indeed, most of the people who had worked on the theoretical foundation of the weapon were not Americans. It seemed obvious to me that the splitting of the atom had created an historical divide. I had no idea what it meant, but I knew that the world would not be the same again. I felt sorrier for myself than for the victims of Hiroshima and Nagasaki.

In the years I attended high school and college, the bomb blended into the landscape, always mentioned, never seen. Despite the endless disarmament conferences held at the height of the Cold War, conventional wisdom held that we would never get rid of it and that it would "never"—they meant "never again"—be used in war. The nuclear arms race that had been accurately predicted by the nuclear scientists was now a fact of life. I remember having conversations with friends about whether we would live a normal life, whether we should have children, whether there was any place to hide. But mostly the horror and fascination of the atomic bomb was submerged somewhere in the subconscious.

I did not begin to think of the atomic bomb as something other than a natural phenomenon until I became conscious of how thoroughly the production, planning, and advertising of nuclear weapons was shot through with deception. The Rosenberg spy trial and their execution appalled me. I assumed that the Rosenbergs were guilty of passing some information to the Russians, though as a law student I thought the evidence flimsy. But the lie that they were responsible for America's vulnerability or for the Korean War, as the judge who condemned them to death solemnly pronounced, was outrageous. The bomb, it seemed to me, was turning the country inside out even while we still had a "monopoly" on the weapon.

James Bryant Conant, the president of Harvard, wrote an article against a "preventive war" on the Soviet Union "now" on the grounds that such a thing would make us look bad and might not be necessary. The idea that there were moral limits standing in the way of exterminating millions of innocent people, if prudent statecraft should so require, was not discussed except in obscure periodicals. I wondered what kind of civilization we were defending with this bomb.

In 1948 or 1949, *Colliers,* a mass circulation magazine of the time, devoted an entire issue to a grisly fantasy of America's atomic victory over the Soviet Union. After a few dozen bombs were dropped, if I recall correctly, the American military government parachuted into the vast remnant of the Soviet empire with copies of Thomas Jefferson and Benjamin Franklin and proceeded to reeducate the entire country in capitalism and democracy. It was as clear a statement of U.S. war aims as could be found at the time, and it made about as much sense as most of the official predictions about the outcome of the nuclear arms race.

I did not really begin to concern myself with the issue of nuclear weapons in a serious way until 1959, when I returned to Harvard for a research project at the Russian Research Center. I had found that spending my day in a rather stuffy Boston law firm, inventing ways for healthy dowagers to keep their income high and their taxes low, offered me something less than what I was looking for. Marshall Shulman, who ran the Russian Research Center at the time, suggested that I do a study of Soviet "negotiating behavior" in the disarmament talks. To do this political science exercise required also looking at U.S. "negotiating behavior."

I had assumed that the USSR used the disarmament issue for propaganda, but I had no idea that the United States played the same game. I accepted the conventional notion that of course the United States wanted disarmament with reliable safeguards—why wouldn't we?—but that the devious, pathologically suspicious, hostile Russians blocked every sensible proposal we put forward.

I went through the entire disarmament debates between 1945 and 1960, and read everything on the subject I could get my hands on. I found out that in May 1955 Harold Stassen, the U.S. disarmament negotiator, had come close to reaching an agreement with the Soviets based to a great extent on U.S. proposals, and that Secretary of State Dulles had flown to London in a panic and blocked the agreement. He fired Stassen and put a "reservation" on all previous U.S. positions. This was not the only example of "negotiating behavior" on our side that suggested more interest in propaganda than in eliminating nuclear weapons. Both sides, I concluded in my study, were playing the same game, although as the weaker power the Soviets, it seemed to me, evinced a greater self-interest in limiting nuclear arms than did the United States. They operated with a clear perception of economic limits. In those heady days, we felt bound by none.

Harvard refused to publish my study for reasons that were never made clear. The Beacon Press did publish *Who Wants Disarmament?* and it received generally favorable reviews and a certain amount of attention. On the strength of the book, I landed a job in Washington with the new Kennedy administration, first in the State Department and then in the new Arms Control and Disarmament Agency.

These two years transformed what had been an intellectual interest accompanied by vague feelings of disquiet into the great concern of my life. I had expected the people on the inside to take the problem of nuclear disarmament seriously, but it was clear from my first week in Washington that, except for a handful of dedicated people in subordinate positions, they did not. I was the secretary on a panel on "new ideas" in disarmament on which sat Henry Kissinger, Paul Nitze, and other eminent national security types. Their interest seemed to be entirely in beating the Soviets in the propaganda battles while leaving the United States free to pursue its own weapons development plans.

Once again I felt deceived. Like most Americans, I had believed the election propaganda put forward by Kennedy about the "missile gap." I soon discovered that the gap existed only in reverse. The United States had an overwhelming "superiority" of all sorts of nuclear weapons. The illusion persisted that we could find a way to "use" these weapons to make the Russians "behave" without having to drop them. But we shouldn't shrink from dropping them.

One Saturday morning during the Berlin crisis of 1961, when I was the duty officer, I saw a cable from the president of the United States to the Berlin commander outlining the circumstances on which he would be authorized to use nuclear weapons. It was one thing to read the grisly "scenarios" of the nuclear strategists about how a nuclear war might start, and quite another to read precise instructions from the president of the United States to a military commander in possession of nuclear weapons on when and where to explode them. The language was no different from that used in a thousand cables I had seen in the government, but these five or six paragraphs of bureaucratic prose could start the chain reaction that could end the world. Nothing in the cable traffic suggested that either the sender or the receiver of the message knew or cared.

I found the bureaucratic machine charged with thinking about national security to be impervious to reason. I listened while distinguished scientists who counseled a sort of freeze of nuclear weapons were charged with advocating "unilateral disarmament."

I remember a meeting to discuss possible war strategies: someone at the meeting expressed concern about the number of casualties that would occur in a war, and one beefy admiral screamed, "If all you're interested in is saving lives, you can always surrender!" In the pastel, windowless offices in the interior corridors of the State Department, Executive Office Building, and Pentagon, where such conversations went on, the dominant note was neither awe nor sorrow but arrogance.

The Christian faith was becoming important in my life. The foolishness of God—that men and women could live in the world without destroying or threatening to destroy one another, that security could never be found in planning for mass murder—was a surer anchor than the "realism" that seemed to lead only to more fear and eventual annihilation. I began to see that the way of the national security manager was not only irrational but blasphemous. Ignorant men were taking delight in playing God, musing about how they were going to blow up whole nations to "punish" some Communist leader. War games, war plans, and all the paraphernalia of bureaucratic homicide I began to see as symptoms of a profound spiritual sickness that had overtaken our country and much of the rest of the world. Yet it was in my country where the sickness was most advanced, for we alone had actually used the bomb, and we were the pace-setters in the arms race.

One day an Air Force general came to demonstrate the new early warning system. "With this new technology," the general said proudly, "I can give the president of the United States an extra seven minutes to decide whether to launch the missiles and bombers of our Strategic Air Command." There was no way to argue with the man or his system, to make him see that he was offering illusion instead of security. The biblical language of idolatry made far more sense as a description of what was happening than the language of nuclear strategy. There was no way out of the race to destruction except somehow to transcend it.

Within the hermetic system of nuclear rationality, there were no solutions. Every good idea for disarmament had its own equally plausible objection. We needed a change of heart as a people before our leaders could feel free enough to change their minds and reject the conventional wisdom of aggressive nationalism. The idea of *metanoia* became much more important in my thinking.

It was not just *what* we thought and felt about security that had to change, but *how* we thought about it. When Einstein said at the dawn of the atomic age that everything had changed but our ways of thinking, he was posing an essentially religious challenge. I saw how easily national security managers separated the compartments of their lives, storing their values in one place, their emotions in another, and their ideas somewhere else. *Metanoia* meant bringing the three together in an effort to see the world as God sees it.

The idea that profound conversion was necessary before a sane national security policy was possible made me very uncomfortable and still does. It has been so easy for defenders of the status quo to profess their love of peace, but to continue preparing for war "until human nature changes." But the process of change takes place in many ways. It need not be an apocalyptical event, though I have heard more than one nuclear scientist express the deeply disturbing view that human beings will not give up the nuclear illusion until bombs are actually exploded in war. Yet to believe that human beings cannot learn without actually experimenting with nuclear war is to reject faith, for the outcome is not likely to be one "limited" nuclear war, but a succession of them leading quite possibly to extinction.

Our genetic forebears have made extraordinary adaptations in the past. Overcoming the nuclear illusion may require a change in our collective behavior as fundamental as moving from a watery environment to dry land. To me, the biblical message is that this historic generation, which has been entrusted with the power to end all life, is commanded to commit itself to the salvation of the human family and our leasehold, the earth.

James Douglass

A Nonviolent Activist

"Three incompetent prayer commandos" is what we called ourselves after our first attempt to pray at a nuclear weapons bunker, on October 30, 1979. Rosemary Powers, John Clark, and I had entered the Trident submarine base in darkness, scrambling over a barbed-wire fence and into heavy brush at the side of a patrol road. A few moments later, the searchlight from a passing security truck flashed onto our bodies stretched out in the brush, paused with its light directly on us, then finally moved on.

We continued our way into the trees of Naval Submarine Base Bangor, Washington state's ground zero—home port for "the ultimate first-strike weapon," as the Trident submarine is described by its former missile-designer, Bob Aldridge. Our objective, whose absurdity corresponded well with our commando incompetence, was to pray inside the Strategic Weapons Facility Pacific (SWFPAC), the nuclear weapons storage area at the center of the base.

Shielded from public view by 7,000 heavily wooded acres of the base, SWFPAC is a barren plot of land with rows of large, earth-covered bunkers which contain Polaris nuclear warheads (and beginning in 1981, Trident warheads). Because of its bunkers' contents, SWFPAC has high-intensity lighting, double security fences, and is patrolled 24 hours a day by Marines armed with dumdum bullets and authorized to use "deadly force."

Our plan was to walk through Bangor's woods, crossing six roads patrolled by naval security, and eventually climb over SWFPAC's two high-security fences in order to pray at "the physical site of an evil we all refuse to see, and thus refuse to take responsibility for"—as we put it in our advance leaflet to the Marines, passed out at the base three weeks earlier. My friends and I formed an "affinity group" whose action was the final stage of a three-day demonstration at the Trident base involving 3,000 people, with more than 100 doing civil disobedience.

In the course of our pilgrimage to SWFPAC, we spent 12 hours undetected on the base, continuously pursued by helicopters, civilian security guards, the Naval Investigative Service, and hundreds of Marines as we climbed fences and crawled through the brush. On two occasions we almost walked into Marine security guards who were looking away from us.

We were finally arrested near a conventional weapons site just short of the high-security fences of SWFPAC. A guard radioed in "V-Day," security trucks converged quickly on the scene, and a helicopter did a long, low victory swoop overhead—"Just like Vietnam except they used bullets there," a naval officer laughed while searching us.

Praying at SWFPAC remains a goal of Ground Zero, the center of nonviolent action alongside the Trident base of which Rosemary, John, and I are members. A month after our first attempt in October, we announced in our weekly leaflet to the base that:

> Ground Zero was founded two years ago to maintain a continuous nonviolent presence at Bangor. We see the effort to go to nuclear storage sites, in a prayerful, nonviolent way, as a central part of that purpose.
>
> Future directions at Ground Zero include our trying again to reach SWFPAC, and in being prepared to give nonviolence training to others to do the same. Our policy at Ground Zero is to resist nuclear weapons by becoming present at their maintenance and storage sites as well as other locations on Bangor, to make nuclear weapons visible and thus intolerable.

The nuclear weapons stored at Bangor, 15 miles across Puget Sound from Seattle, have created a deepening moral conflict between the United States Navy and nonviolent resisters. If resisters should persist in trying to climb high-security fences to nuclear weapons storage sites, at Bangor or anywhere else, injury or loss of life is probable—not a nonviolent conclusion. Moreover, such an act of violence would in some sense be "forced" on security people following apparently reasonable orders to protect nuclear weapons. What is there in the nature of nonviolence or nuclear weapons which creates a situation in which good people may in conscience end up shooting other good people acting in conscience in a provocative way?

A beginning response to that question comes in a reflection by a man who lost two daughters in the mass suicides at Jonestown:

> Death reigned when there was no one free enough, nor strong enough, nor filled with rage enough, to run and throw his body against a vat of cyanide, spilling it on the ground. Are there people free enough and strong enough who will throw themselves against the vats of nuclear stockpiles for the sake of the world? Without such people, hundreds of millions of human beings will consume the nuclear cyanide, and it will be murder. Our acquiescence in our own death will make it suicide.

But this image is deceptively simple compared to the possibilities for action amid the stark realities of SWFPAC: Throwing one's self against the concrete slab door of a bunker might fracture some bones but it won't break the hypnotic spell nuclear weapons have over America.

After reflecting on the absurdity of the situation—what does one *do* in the presence of an H-bomb?—we decided that the only thing we could do was to go to SWFPAC, in a pilgrimage to that point of responsibility. Once there, we could only ask God's forgiveness and mercy for our responsibility in creating such weapons, and pray for the power to be transformed in our collective conscience to a responsible, loving people capable of disarmament. Our meditations on the futility of any direct action we could take inside SWFPAC, in the presence of such instruments of mass murder, helped us realize again the profound miracles called for today in human hearts and institutions if nuclear war is to be stopped.

Our seven-person affinity group, which we called "Luna" after a feminine reality we hoped to embody, recognized that our preparation for the action part lay not only in nonviolent techniques but in community reflection and prayer. We had to prepare ourselves for the possibility of being shot.

The clear way in which death, or being maimed, was discussed and accepted by the seven of us (especially difficult in the case of the four who had the task of waiting in support outside the base fence) seemed a miracle in itself—in an anti-nuclear movement which like its culture avoids the demands and consequences of nonviolence.

If any of us were shot, we expected sharp repudiation of our action from members of that movement who would like our lives to be given not at all or at least more effectively than in an absurd prayer. But we had worse feelings about the reaction of religious friends who might choose to deform us into something unique rather than see a simple invitation to themselves to take their own further steps into nonviolent awareness and responsibility.

Of deep concern to us were the Marines on the other side of SWFPAC's fences, who had the contradictory responsibility of guarding nuclear weapons. The leaflet we addressed to them three weeks before the action was meant to give them time to think before shooting. After stating our intention to pray where the weapons were, we said:

> We know that it is your responsibility to guard these nuclear sites. We ask you to consider carefully in advance our attempt to join you there. We know that by government regulations you are "authorized to use deadly force" in protecting nuclear weapons. Brothers, we ask instead that you lay down your arms, for the sake of all our lives. We know that you are good people, and that you love and respect life.

Prayer and the hope expressed in our leaflet did not, however, overcome personal fears. We had been told repeatedly by the base that the Marines were under strict orders to shoot on sight any SWFPAC intruders. If we succeeded in reaching and climbing SWFPAC fences, we expected to be shot—and reasonably so.

Shooting SWFPAC intruders is reasonable if one begins with the government's premises. Ground Zero's view that nuclear weapons are a larger form of Jonestown's vats of cyanide is countered by the government's position that nuclear weapons are the source of U.S. security.

Over a 34-year period, this government premise has resulted in the stockpiling of 30,000 nuclear weapons distributed throughout the world in high-security storage sites such as SWFPAC. The spread of such weapons, with the increasing threat of their passing into terrorist hands, has emphasized the need for heightened security measures. It is clear that city-destroying warheads justify the use of "deadly force" against intruders (whose nonviolent credentials can't be examined as they climb high-security fences). If one accepts the government's premise, it follows that SWFPAC intruders should be shot on sight.

Why, then, weren't we shot on October 30?

The outcome of that first attempt to enter SWFPAC illustrates the contradictions of a nuclear-based democracy:

We weren't shot, first of all, because we didn't reach the nuclear storage sites. But as we were driven in security vans past our intended destination, a deeper answer to that question was revealed. We saw that SWFPAC's nuclear-weapons-storage site had been emptied of all military, civilian, and contracting personnel, and had been left with its double gates wide open. While every available Bangor security force had been out hunting us all day, SWFPAC had been evacuated on the chance that we might reach our goal— so that if we did, we could enter the area without being shot under the usual standing security orders. If we had reached SWFPAC, we would have been able to walk through open gates to a nonviolent arrest.

One reason, we believe, for this unusual response is that the people at Bangor are indeed "good people, who love and respect life." They are people who know us at Ground Zero, after our having passed out leaflets to them for 60 consecutive weeks; people who know that we respect them. We gave the Marines and their command three weeks' notice to think before shooting. We believe that the base commander's orders at SWFPAC reflected a more widespread unwillingness to shoot us.

A second, more political reason for the sweeping revision of SWFPAC security is the government's need to keep the lid tight on that vat of nuclear cyanide we were trying to knock over into the public conscience. Invisibility of nuclear weapons is indispensable to their retention in a democracy. Our collective nuclear insanity rests on political conditions, the first of which is a people's lack of awareness that life itself is at stake. The American people will not tolerate nuclear weapons once our collective eyes are opened to their implications. That was the democratic logic of our effort to climb SWFPAC's fences—and government authorities understood.

Growing terrorism from abroad and from within is the inevitable consequence of a nuclear arms race we have led since August 6, 1945. The government has recognized this for some time; hence its gradual policy shift from a nuclear deterrent strategy, designed to prevent nuclear war in a world controlled by two superpowers, to a nuclear counterforce or first-strike strategy, designed to fight and "win" a nuclear war against anyone in a multinuclear world where deterrence is no longer possible—the world of the 1980s.

The government, as a system of power based on nuclear weapons since 1945, has recognized the implications of those weapons for some time. But the people have not. By our pilgrimage to Bangor's ground zero, we were attempting to open our collective eyes to the life-and-death reality in our midst. Because the government recognized our intention, it took the extreme measure of suspending its usual nuclear-site security of deadly force for a period of three days (the length of our larger demonstration) to arrest us without alerting the public conscience to the seriousness of what we were probing.

But nonviolence as a way of life, which is Ground Zero's purpose, has a characteristic which has heightened the conflict with the navy at SWFPAC: tenacity.

Less than one month after our first pilgrimage, we handed out a leaflet with a qualifying note absent from the statements on our first attempt:

> This leaflet is our public announcement of our intention to act again at SWFPAC in the future—at some day and hour for which we will give no further notice. We hope this kind of nonviolent action can deepen and spread. We share it with you today as our pledge to deepen in nonviolence in a way that might begin to correspond to the depth of the nuclear crisis.

Nuclear weapons, and their security measures, remain when mass demonstrations are over. The test of nonviolence is to maintain its commitment just as steadily as our friends in the military maintain their commitment. Ground Zero hopes to touch Bangor's moral nerve at SWFPAC every day of the year by attempting to go there periodically without giving the base advance notice of particular dates that would allow it to waive security measures.

A fundamental teaching of Gandhi was that all persons

should hold on to their deepest beliefs to the end, carrying their actions to the ultimate consequences of their beliefs. Such a process admittedly heightens conflict; but it also results in a new and transforming truth for all the parties in a conflict.

Those who believe in the government's premise that nuclear weapons are our source of security, however insecure that security, have a more basic premise—a deeper belief—that nonviolent change to a nuclear-free world is impossible, or so remote a possibility as to make necessary our deepening nuclear gamble for security. The deeper belief in nuclear weapons is actually despair. The premise behind the bomb, and all its implications, is despair of nonviolent change.

No one believes in nuclear weapons as such, but many Americans have given up hope of reversing the world's (and our own) reliance on them. Thus for the sake of security the premise of the "real world" carries with it the escalating threat of nuclear weapons and all the heightened security measures necessary to protect the weapons from terrorists: SWFPAC intruders should be shot on sight. A belief in nuclear weapons demands it.

To those who continue to believe deeply in that position after examining its implications, Gandhi would say: So be it. Live your truth through to its conclusion. Given the unchangeable reality you see, you are right to build the weapons and right to defend them to the death. (Gandhi would also hope that such nuclear believers would be resisted out of love by others.)

For those who see a different reality, one in which a nuclear-free world is truly possible, different actions are called for. Gandhi called them "experiments in truth," tentative, searching efforts to discover and carry through actions which will intensify a conflict in truth and ultimately open it up. If, for example, you truly believe that we're now living in a global Jonestown and that a different world is possible, then bet your life on the truth of climbing SWFPAC's fences to spill those nuclear vats across the public conscience, to awaken us as a people from insanity to responsibility. Let the "real world" beliefs of those who defend SWFPAC's weapons against terrorists, and the hope-filled beliefs of nonviolent resisters who see the terror as already there, meet as conflicting truths at those fences.

On the Feast of the Epiphany, January 6, 1980, our Luna affinity group sought to pray again at nuclear bunkers. Two of us,

John Clark and I, entered the Trident base at 6 in the morning. We hiked through the base woods all day, spotting occasional patrol trucks in the distance, until darkness stopped us.

That night, while sitting in thick woods and 20-degree weather a few hundred feet from nuclear bunkers, we thanked God for the gift of being brought there and wondered at the next day's events. We were sustained in that all-night vigil by the love and prayers of our affinity group and by more distant friends with whom we felt at one.

The next morning we used stepping stools and rug remnants to climb over the 12-foot-high double security fences enclosing SWFPAC. The slanted barbed wire at the top of the fences ripped open my down-filled winter jacket in more than 20 places, giving the scene we left behind the appearance of a raided chicken coop: stepping stools abandoned by the fences, carpets piled across the barbed wire, and feathers billowing up everywhere.

We walked alone and unimpeded to the first nuclear bunker. It was like a tomb—huge sliding concrete slabs shut under a small mountain of earth. We stood in silence for several minutes on the concrete entry, joined hands, and said aloud the Lord's Prayer and the Hail Mary. Then we walked on to the next bunker, and prayed there in the same way. We continued our nuclear Stations of the Cross for six bunkers before we were arrested. At the second bunker we noticed that a security patrol truck had parked a short distance away and was watching us. However, for whatever reason, the guards in the truck allowed us to continue our prayer at four more bunkers.

We were confronted finally at the sixth bunker by a construction worker in a truck and by a variety of security guards, including Marines carrying their rifles in readiness. All were remarkably peaceful.

Later we were charged simply with illegally re-entering the Trident base. A base spokesperson issued a public statement saying there were no nuclear weapons in the specific bunkers we had prayed at. As for there being nuclear weapons in SWFPAC: "We can neither confirm nor deny that."

We are continuing to work with other affinity groups who plan pilgrimages to the nuclear bunkers in SWFPAC.

Virginia Ramey Mollenkott

A Feminist

Disturbed by what seemed to me to be a lack of long-range planning or concern on his part, I asked my twenty-four-year-old son, "What would you like to be doing with your life when you are fifty, my age?"

He looked at me in astonishment. "Why, Mother, I'm never going to *see* fifty!"

I felt a thud in the pit of my stomach, afraid that he had presentiments of some dread disease that I knew nothing about. When I rallied my nerve to ask for an explanation, he spoke with exaggerated patience: "Don't you know that the Lord is coming soon, and after we Christians are taken out of here, the world will be destroyed by nuclear bombs?" He glanced around the restaurant where we were sitting: "Nobody *in here* is going to be around for very long."

Recognizing the influence of his grandmother, his father, and his uncle, I cast about for ways to respond without seeming to smear their honor. I also needed time to absorb the jolting realization that expectations of nuclear destruction explained some of the apathy, hedonism, and suicidal despair among some of the young people in my college classes. And I remembered.

I remembered that my own grandmother's favorite Bible verse was Nahum 1:7: "The Lord is good, a stronghold in the day of trouble, and he knows those who take refuge in him." Another favorite of hers was Isaiah 31:1: "Woe to those who go down to Egypt for help and rely on horses, who trust in chariots . . . but do not look to the Holy One of Israel. . . ." The third in her triumvirate of protection passages was Zechariah 4:6: "Not by might, nor by power, but by my Spirit, says the Lord of hosts."

Unfortunately, however, what operated with great strength in her personal faith seemed to have no relevance concerning the larg-

112

er society—not for my grandmother, and not for the family she ruled as matriarch. While our personal protection might stem from the Lord of hosts, we never questioned that the United States ought to look out for us by might and by power. Apparently, God's Spirit could be expected to operate only in the private sphere. For international safety, one must trust in the modern equivalent of Isaiah's chariots and horses: military force based on lots of sophisticated and expensive weapons, the more the better. They were the *means* God would use to keep us American Christians safe and superior.

I remembered that at our Gospel Chapel, there were often speakers who painstakingly explained huge charts of the dispensations and the "end times." Things would grow worse and worse in this world, we were told, until suddenly Christ would return, the world would be destroyed in a dreadful conflagration, and a New Heaven and New Earth would be established under the rule of God. For proof, there were biblical texts like 2 Peter 3:10–13: "But the day of the Lord will come like a thief, and then the heavens will pass away with a loud noise, and the elements will be dissolved with fire, and the earth and the works that are upon it will be burned up."

I was thirteen when the first atomic bomb was dropped, and three times in my adulthood I have dreamed vividly of my own demise in nuclear fallout. My imagination was fueled by Plymouth Brethren preachers who very soon capitalized on the fact that the devastating effects of the bomb seemed a good match for the details in passages like 2 Peter 3:10–13. The possibility of a worldwide atomic disaster was almost welcomed at our Gospel Chapel. After all, it provided the scientific method by which biblical prophecies could come true.

Inevitably, inasmuch as there was any consideration of an ethical stance toward atomic warfare, the stance was one of *laissez-faire*. What would be the point of struggling against the stockpiling of weapons, what would be the sense in seeking global harmony, when the total destruction of the world was inevitable anyhow? People's saying "Peace, peace, when there is no peace" was surely a sign of the end times. Pacifists were therefore the objects of deep suspicion, possibly even forerunners of the antichrist.

Sitting across the table from my son, who could not think about his future because for him the world had no future, I remembered all this. More than the restaurant table separated us, I realized. A whole set of assumptions about the nature of God, human-kind, and the natural creation separated us. Yet there was a time when I had sat where he was sitting. What had moved me from that position to my present one?

Many factors, of course. One of them was my journey toward personal liberation. I had been taught that as a woman, my role was to be secondary to and supportive of all men in general, and my husband in particular. And I had tried my best to shrink myself to the size of that role. But I became bewildered by the fact that the more submissive I tried to be, the more I was taken for granted, used up, stepped on. Finally, one despairing day, I faced the fact that my course was one of psychological suicide. Had God really created and gifted me with the intention of crushing the life out of all that I was potentially meant to be? In my heart I could not accept that thought, and I began to read and study and take steps toward the fulfillment of my destiny in Christ Jesus.

What was true for me, personally, I later reasoned, was true for the creation as a whole. God had not created and gifted and provided redemption for the world only in order to destroy all of its reality and all of its potential.

As an emerging feminist whose doctorate was in the art of reading with care and precision, I discovered that when reading contextually, the Bible contains a strong theme of male-female equality and indeed a theme of human unity through creation and redemption. I learned that realization of that profound oneness or unity is meant to melt all barriers, whether those barriers are ra-cial, sexual, orientational, economic, or nationalistic.

In this connection, I was moved by an essay by psychologist R. D. Laing on "Us and Them," and especially by this sentence: "We are 'they' to them and they are 'they' to us." I reasoned that if we got caught up in the destruction of "them," we were actually getting caught up in the destruction of ourselves. People in the So-viet Union inevitably think of Americans as "them," just as surely as we Americans regard Soviets as "them," with this important difference: that America has actually dropped atomic bombs, whereas the Soviet Union has not. (It felt so strange to me to real-ize that my own dearly loved United States is feared around the world as a tremendously violent nation.) I felt that Laing's insight concerning us and them was accurate even in the era of convention-al weapons; but with the development of nuclear weapons that did not distinguish between combatants and noncombatants, the impossibility of distinguishing us from them became *overwhelmingly* true. Having turned my back on psychological suicide, I was not drawn toward the idea of global suicide.

It occurred to me that if "the difference between men and boys is the price of their toys," then nuclear weapons are the ultimate toy with the ultimate price tag: the destruction of Mother Earth. I began to notice a distinct correlation between attitudes of male supremacy and an attraction to weapons, including support of the nuclear arms race. As an evangelical, I was especially disturbed to realize that the then-emerging Religious Right coupled its claims to being biblical with a whole constellation of interests that are patriarchal in the extreme, and all of them oriented toward death.

While opposing equal rights for women and protecting the right of the family patriarch to punish "his" children with impunity, the Religious Right supports unrestrained profit economics, the death penalty, ever-increased military spending, and the expansion of nuclear power. So I came to realize that male primacy in the home and church breeds the idea that dominance is acceptable and necessary in the larger society. Thus it breeds the dominance of the rich within the nation and the dominance of military and economic might between nations.

In this way, I came to realize that the perversion of male-female equal partnership contributes heavily to the armed-camp atmosphere of the world. My own experience had taught me that genuine love is always fostered by mutual give-and-take, while dominant *power-over* fosters only resentment in the oppressed and guilt in the oppressor. But I came to realize that these effects operate just as much between nations as they do between individual persons. The rigidities of hierarchy have brought the world only a push-button (or a computer error) away from rigor mortis for the whole human race.

At last I came to the point at which I knew that those who support male primacy in the home and church are only being true to themselves when they also support the oppression of the poor on the national level and the dominance of economic and military muscle on the international scene. Although a few might *partially* break that pattern, the trend of patriarchy seems to me to be hell-bent on self-destruction. As a biblical feminist, I choose flexible growth rather than rigid status quo, equality and mutuality rather than hierarchy, life rather than death.

The hope that keeps my vision of global harmony alive is the biblical theme that God intends, through human agency empowered by the Holy Spirit, to bring the whole creation under the loving sovereignty of the Christ (Ephesians 3:10 and elsewhere). I believe that it is possible for individuals and nations to learn to serve one another's best interests in mutuality out of reverence for the new humanity embodied in Jesus. On the practical level, that would mean learning to solve differences by negotiation rather than by warfare and threats of warfare. I know, of course, that such statements sound preposterous to the ears of those who have internalized patriarchal ideas about what provides security and what legitimates exploitation. Nevertheless, I believe that *metanoia* is always possible as long as life remains. We *can* be transformed by the renewal of our minds. We *can* learn that, even in the twentieth century, security stems from doing justice and loving mercy and walking humbly with God.

Several years ago, I began to learn existentially what it *means* that perfect love casts out fear (1 John 4:18). Because fear is the opposite of love, they cannot coexist. As I have grown in the ability to love, I have felt various longstanding fears melting away from me. Indeed, I have found that to the degree that I love, I do not fear, and to the degree that I fear, I do not love. And I have learned to deeply *know* this: that like racism, sexism, heterosexism, and economic elitism, the arms race is an expression of fear. By basing our sense of national security on weaponry, we consistently reinforce our own fear of being attacked. The more we try to dominate the world by flexing our military muscles, the more we ourselves feel threatened, because in our hearts we know how empty such posturing really is. Hence, there never *could* be enough weapons to satisfy us. The more weapons we build, the more we stimulate the fear that makes us think we need still more weapons.

The snarl of the cornered cur stems from fear. The swagger of the bully stems from fear. Macho insolence and brutality toward women stems from fear. Security can come only through trusting the love of God and obeying the biblical principle of respectful mutuality between human beings, between humankind and nature, and between nations. Although our patriarchal world adores economic and military might, we need not conform ourselves to this world.

We can learn to do justice to one another out of reverence for the One in whom all of us live and move and have our being (Acts 17:28).

I wish I could close with the report that I was able to convince my son of all that I have written here. I wish I could tell you that he had come to the realization that by expecting the human race to be swallowed up in a nuclear holocaust, he was contributing to energy toward that kind of disaster. Instead, all I can report is that he seems to be living his life more purposefully these days and seems to be planning more confidently toward a meaningful future. The energy he contributes to the world is more positive than it used to be. So is mine. And for these changes, I am grateful.

John Perkins

A Community Organizer

Since my conversion in 1957, I have struggled with what it means to be a Christian. I realized that I must be as much like Christ as I can be, that the "out living" of the "in living" Christ must be portrayed in my life. Galatians 2:20 made a great impression on me. There Paul says, "I have been crucified with Christ, it is no longer I who live, but Christ who lives in me; and the life I now live in the flesh I live by faith in the Son of God, who loved me and gave himself for me."

Another passage of Scripture that has shaped my Christian life is Hebrews 4:12–13, which says, "For the word of God is living and active, sharper than any two-edged sword, piercing to the division of soul and spirit, of joints and marrow, and discerning the thoughts and intentions of the heart. And before him no creature is hidden but all are open and laid bare to the eyes of him with whom we have to do."

My opposition to war and the nuclear buildup has to do with my environment and my struggle with what it means to be a Christian. These verses have been a means by which I have struggled to apply what I learned both from the word of God, and from what I sensed to be the need of the society in which I found myself.

I was brought up on a plantation in Mississippi in much poverty, but with a lot of hope that life would improve. My mother died when I was seven months old. My father gave his five children to his mother, who was already the mother of nineteen. I didn't have much of an opportunity to go to school or any encouragement from home to study hard. As a black person on a plantation, I had no example of what it would look like to get a good education and lead a successful life. Thus, I dropped out of school between the third and fifth grades.

When World War II came, I saw my uncles and brothers go

into the military, and to us this represented hope that life would someday be better. We hoped that our poverty would someday end and that the injustice that was inflicted against us as a people would cease. We were very aware during those years of how wrong things were.

My teacher, Miss Maybelle Armstrong, taught us black songs and instilled within us a love for our people and their struggles. We learned about what they had accomplished, and we gained a love for those who had struggled on behalf of black people. We studied about Booker T. Washington and Frederick Douglass who became my heroes. Statements like, "There are no attributes of God that can agree with oppression" made deep imprints on my life as I watched the oppression inflicted upon our people in the little town of New Hebron, where I grew up.

One of our young men who went off to service returned to New Hebron wearing his uniform, probably feeling very good about being home. The whites beat him up, as they beat up many of our people right in the streets. Back in those days, on a Saturday afternoon, many would come to town to walk the streets. We often wondered what would have happened if the military had come in and defended that young man, but they never came.

From that time on, many blacks began to move away from New Hebron. They left for many reasons. There were job opportunities because of the war, jobs like building the airport and hospital in Jackson and the military bases around Jackson. Some of our boys went to Hattiesburg to work, helping to build the army camp for the war. All of this brought hope. And when our people came back, they had money for the first time.

So the war became a symbol of hope. With our boys going into the service, we began to get a newspaper so we could read about what was going on overseas in the war. We also gained hope from black star athletes. During the war there was Joe Louis, and after the war, Jackie Robinson. As they defeated white people as well as black people, they gave us a desire to succeed.

When my brother and cousin came back to New Hebron after the war, my brother was killed by a white marshal and my cousin was killed by his wife. Our family made plans to move away from our little town. Cotton was disappearing as a main source of work and livelihood for us in the rural areas. The standard of living had increased, and our little farms could no longer support the families.

Many rushed away to the big thriving cities of the North, but my family went to California.

In 1957 I was converted to Christ. I was converted in the midst of a fundamental Bible movement and became part of the Christian Business Men Committee, Child Evangelism Fellowship, and a small Holiness Church. At this time I began to study the dispensational truths.

As I began to read and study the Bible, I started to understand it because the dispensationalists did a good job of rightly dividing the Word of truth. But I became aware of the fact that there was some of the Bible that we did not emphasize and did not take as applicable truth. We believed it as historical truth, we believed it as a future blessing that could happen, but we did not take, for example, the Sermon on the Mount or the twenty-fifth chapter of Matthew as applying to our lives. That was to be delayed to a future time when Jesus would return to set up his kingdom.

In 1960, three years after my conversion, I went back to my home state of Mississippi. I found that the poverty there was great, but I also found that the poverty of the spirit was just as great. I discovered that our churches were locked into a tradition and that the people were not concerned about reaching other people for Christ. They had the idea that some day, if the lost would come to church, they would change; some day they would get through this period that they were going through.

I lived in the little town of Mendenhall and began to study the poverty. I saw that many of our young girls were pregnant by the time they were fifteen years of age. Their chances and opportunities were cut, and they found themselves locked into poverty.

Many of our people were locked into poverty in spite of their own aspirations. They would talk about the whites, who oppressed them and who enslaved them, with a greater excitement than they talked about their own people. When they talked about their own people, it would be with a degenerated attitude. I came to understand what had happened to us as a people. It was like Malcolm X had said, they had come "to love their master more than they loved themselves."

I saw that most of the white ministers in my town were indifferent. I watched one of my white friends, a pastor of a local church, commit suicide because he had begun to be aware and wanted to do something about the oppression and poverty around him. I watched the indifference of the local black pastors to the civil rights movement, and noted that they felt threatened. There was, in fact, some threat. The white people were burning black churches.

I watched the Ku Klux Klan as it developed around us with its patriotism and anticommunism. I heard speeches by people like Senator Eastland, who had been to South Africa and who spoke strongly against those "rebels," those "communists" who were trying to overthrow the government of South Africa. I knew how oppressive the South African government was, and I wanted to overthrow the Mississippi government myself.

Each year I would come back to California, and I began to see that my dispensational friends had a concern about my soul, but not about the physical environment in which I found myself. I was concerned about my soul, but my soul had peace with God. That's what I had received when I found Jesus. I felt peace with God. But my body was still in slavery.

In 1969, I met a man from the Brethren Volunteer Service. He had come to Mississippi to visit me, and told me that he wanted to speak in the local high school about war and peace. I had become aware of the war in Vietnam and what that meant to our people. He spoke at our school, Harper High School; the principal was not there. This man spoke about the fact that young people should not go to Vietnam, should not go to war. I remember him offering to counsel with young men who did not want to go into the military.

But the military, for these young men, had been hope. It offered a job and a way to get out of Mississippi. It offered an opportunity to explore the world that they would not otherwise have. So when this man from the Brethren Church spoke, some of the young people grew hostile.

The principal came to my house when he got back that day, and spoke to me about my Brethren friend. He said, "John, I always let you bring people to the school and speak, but today you threw me a curve ball." I asked him why, and he said that my friend had spoken against war, against the military. I said to him, "Don't you think that it is educational for our young people to hear another's side?" When we came out of that discussion, we were still friends, but it caused me to think more about looking at the other side of the war question and at what the war was doing to us.

The more I looked and compared, and began to meet people from the Mennonite, Brethren, Quaker, and other peace churches as they volunteered to be a part of our work in Mississippi, I found that the peace church people and I could discuss issues and there could be disagreements, but we could still maintain our relationship. But with other people, evangelical and dispensationalist people, I saw that when I disagreed with them it created a sense of alienation. And I did not want that alienation, because learning the dispensational tradition had meant a lot to me in terms of understanding the Bible.

I tried to maintain a relationship with my Mennonite, Brethren, and Quaker friends, and at the same time with those people who had meant so much to me in sharing with me the Word of Life. It was my desire to hang onto that which was good within the dispensational tradition, and at the same time try to receive more and become more involved with people from the peace movement.

All this created a struggle. I was living in bondage and slavery in Mississippi. I wanted freedom and justice. The legend of Martin Luther King and his teaching on nonviolence hung on. I was involved in cooperative economic development, and the people in that cooperative movement began to question the level of military spending over against the poverty with which we were trying to deal in Mississippi. I found myself in Mississippi trying to maintain and cultivate the best in the dispensational movement, while at the same time trying to be the body of Christ here on earth; trying to hang onto my belief that the Bible was inspired and trying to believe that the whole Bible was to be applied to my life in some way.

In 1970, in the midst of this struggle, came a great turning point in my life: I was almost beaten to death in the Brandon jail by the Mississippi Highway Patrol and the Ku Klux Klan. As they called me a nigger and a communist and beat me, I saw how these poor people, who felt so threatened by communism and by the civil rights movement, had a distorted pride as they carried their guns and maintained the peace through oppression. I saw very clearly what hatred could do to people as I looked into the faces of those policemen. I saw what hatred was doing to my state of Mississippi; it was putting us at the bottom of the barrel.

This experience of seeing the distorted pride these policemen had in carrying their guns caused me to look again at the policemen, the guards, and people who would go into the military. It made me look at what made men beat their wives to maintain a dominant superiority. I looked again at militarism, and what it was doing to people. I saw senators and congressmen who were for military might and military spending but not devoted to Jesus Christ. I saw churches in Mississippi, the white churches, not speaking out against the Vietnam War, not speaking out against militarism, and not speaking out against the poverty in Mississippi. I saw how the oppressive mindset of militarism was crippling us.

So I began to meet people like Ron Sider and Mark Hatfield, who were struggling with some of the same issues. I spoke in colleges and schools and became a part of the Mennonite movement, the Brethren movement, the evangelical movement, the seminary scene, and other scenes.

I began to accept and apply the Sermon on the Mount and the twenty-fifth chapter of Matthew, those passages I had read but dispensationalized to the kingdom age and not applied to my own life here. I began to read afresh that we as believers should struggle to be peacemakers, because Christ says, "Blessed are the peacemakers." I began to understand the incarnated truth that God has brought us into his family through the work of Jesus Christ.

And I want to live out, as much as I can, his life here on earth. I want to be as prophetic as I can be. And I believe that the possibility of war, of nuclear war, is a fearful, fearful thought.

I believe that we who are opposed to military might must be peacemakers not only against military expansion, but must be peacemakers in the community too. We must be in the business of trying to reconcile our religious differences, not in terms of trying to change a church's statement of faith or trying to change denominational positions, but trying to mold a reconciled relationship where we can together be more prophetic. Then we can move against some of the evil and some of the injustice in our society.

I believe that Jesus will return one day and that when he returns, he will make this world what he wants it to be. But in the meantime he wants us to occupy the earth until he comes.

Jesus wants us to be peacemakers, to bring people into that conversion experience where they find peace with God, through our Lord Jesus Christ, and peace of mind. This is where they find that peace which Paul describes as surpassing all understanding, that peace which comes from knowing you have been loved by a holy God and responding to his love. Then we are to work to bring peace between our fellow men and women. Then we can say as the Apostle Paul said, "All this is from God, who through Christ reconciled us to himself and gave us the ministry of reconciliation" (2 Corinthians 5:18).

I want to serve the rest of my life trying to bring reconciliation between the races, a reconciliation which will bring about a movement that will try to deal with the poor and the oppressed and disenfranchised of our world. I even pray that there could be a reconciliation, a working reconciliation, between capitalism and communism and socialism, a reconciliation between these economic and philosophical entities that would concentrate on the poor and disenfranchised, those people who die from malnutrition; that we would understand that these people were created in the image of God, that they have dignity. I know that they have dignity because I was one of those poor and oppressed.

It is my hope that as the rich see their responsibility they will be moved to divest themselves of their excess wealth, maintaining that which is necessary for production and sharing with the poor and oppressed of this world that wealth which goes beyond their needs.

I want to encourage the poor not to depend upon the wealth and benevolence of someone else, but to see themselves as having dignity, to be people who can explore this world and be people like those described by the Apostle Paul, people who work with their own hands so that they themselves can have in order to give to people in need.

Yes, I have come to the place where I believe that we are in fact the keeper of our brother and sister, and that we are to be their keeper until Christ himself returns and takes control of this world. And I believe that we are to affirm human life and human dignity in all of our life's activities.

Elizabeth McAlister
A Member of a Resistance Community

I have become one of the endless stream that passes in and out of prison gates. It is good that I am. It is right that we should know how to suffer (and, if we have already known, that we should not forget); that I am forced to the level of the most miserable of people before I judge others; and that I experience in my heart again and again the sufferings of the dispossessed.

If one is white in an inner-city jail, one stands out from the crowd. This is intensified when one also looks straight, in middle years, and crowned with white hairs. One inmate studied me scrupulously and quite openly before saying: "You don't belong here. You ought to be a wife and mother!" "I am," I said, "and all the more reason why I ought to be here."

The argument is not heredity vs. environment, though each plays a role. I was raised white, middle class, suburban, Irish-Catholic, one of seven children, a twin. By right and duty and training, I should have carried the same banner. What happened? Tolstoy tells a story, "After the Ball," of a man whose whole life was changed after he, quite accidentally, witnessed the brutal beating of a deserter by his brother soldiers. They entered into the inhuman action so totally, he reflected, that they must know something he did not know. And since he was never able to discover what they knew, he could never enter military service, or, as it developed, any other service, because each had its own secrets enabling its members to engage in other inhuman acts. The man became a wandering philosopher.

A few elements stand out in my own pilgrimage. In retrospect, they weave a thread somewhere close to the center of my being. Throughout childhood I sensed an urge to serve people more directly than the wife-mother models around me would allow. Was the urge any more than childhood fantasy? Is childhood fantasy too often ignored in adult life? Religious life, as I perceived it in my teachers, did not answer my longing. But the call from Christ was so insistent that at length I submitted and entered deeply into the silence and prayer of the novitiate. I went into religious community with a love of Scripture and unanswered questions, chief among them the question: To what service was I called?

The change had been subtle: a vague, even naive, sense that citizenship in the kingdom could not be reconciled with citizenship in the Great Society, that rationalizations about containment of communism could not justify widespread killings in war, that Christ and not the presidency (even in its Camelot years) was the way, the truth, and the life.

I was reading the bad news, but had my other eye on the good news. For several years, it was all personal, interior: "Of course the war in Indochina is irreconcilable with the gospels!" I didn't understand all the political implications, but I knew in my soul it was wrong. And, though very inexperienced, I knew the justifications to be congested with falsehood and deception, if not straightforward lies.

I was teaching a class in "Principles of Art Criticism." We were studying Suzanne Langer's theory of symbolic forms. A discussion was in process to determine first whether the students understood what Langer was saying and then what, if any, of her view might be incorporated into their own understanding of art. One student came up with a formulation, and I responded that she was correct. And then she said: "Well if you believe that about art, then you'd support what David Miller just did!" (David Miller was the first public draft card burner. His was, in Langer's understanding, an act of symbolic form. It contained in itself the reality of his resistance and pointed to the profound reality of the evil of the war and the need for resistance to it. It was a profound leap for the student and perfectly on target.) I affirmed what she had said and the connections she had made. The remainder of the class was astonishing. The students tried to convince me of the error of my view about all the forms that I had left behind me (such as the domino theory, the unique goodness of American policies, and communism as totally evil), and naively thought everyone else had abandoned too.

As a result of that one exchange, the floodgates opened: reproaches, rebukes, denunciations, efforts from so many sides to educate me to the real facts of real life, silence and avoidance from others. And from unexpected quarters, a few came rejoicing, nurturing, supporting—a small community, within that religious community, groping like a few others to be responsible to the gospel in a world of war.

Only a few in those days from 1964 to 1965 had roots and perceptions that were Christian or biblical. Innocent, even childlike, we could not comprehend then the length and height and breadth of the violence we were seeking to confront. As the revelation came upon us, slowly, by degrees, each of us had to face personal fear, doubt, despair. Many of us dropped out, many were plucked off along the way. Those of us who remained were forced to dig more deeply into nonviolence, the scriptures, each other. Phil Berrigan and I shared those years. They seemed hard then—then we hardly knew what hard meant—and yet so joyful. We had community within the wider community of the peace movement that, years later, I discovered was a rare gift helping to account for the endurance of so many of us.

Young men resisted the draft and went to jail. What of us? How does one move from dissent to resistance? I recall being bewildered by the question; peacemaking for me was still part-time, an extracurricular activity. Phil took the lead in the transition in October 1967 when, with three brothers, he poured blood on files that made murderers of young men. My response to the action was instantaneous. It was symbolic form; it was sacramental. The action of the "Baltimore Four" became a precedent for four years of work with small groups who wanted to live their beliefs. Some two hundred or more draft board actions occurred; there were innumerable confrontations with courts and judges and jails.

Were the actions symbolic or effective? Through them we became enemies of the state, a threat to its political hegemony. Intimidations, defamation, harassment followed. We were subject to massive prosecution. Big guns aimed to cut off our credibility, if not our future. The Harrisonburg Trial, from 1971 to 1972, was a time of evaluation, reflection, redirection. The war continued unabated, being met more and more by public silence, acceptance, weariness. For resistance to flourish, we faced the need to begin again, to rebuild, reform, over and over and over.

We needed to see to it in our rebuilding that people planted roots deep enough to sustain the long-haul effort. It would require our whole life, perhaps that of our children. We needed to weed out coerciveness as much as we could while keeping urgency alive; to sustain the positive dimension of strong community for the sake of growth and nonviolent resistance. We needed to work so that community would become strong, real, Christian.

After Harrisonburg we began again with a position paper and a small group. A year of hard dialogues, changes, decisions. In June 1973, we opened in Baltimore the community called Jonah House.

In January of 1974, James Schlesinger began to talk about a change in our nuclear policy away from "mutually assured destruction" to what he termed "flexible and strategic targeting options"—in other words, the development of a first-strike capability and a policy that would include first-strike use of nuclear weapons. Some commentators editorialized that this policy made nuclear war inevitable.

We read and discussed these developments in community, and began to have dialogues about altering the focus of our resistance away from the war in Indochina and toward this type of weaponry. We read whatever we could find about what had happened in nuclear weapons development while our focus had been on the war. Our first tentative action against our nuclear weapons and U.S. policy occurred even as the U.S. retreat from Hanoi was in process. In January 1976, we made our first statement against nuclear annihilation at the Pentagon, the first of more than I would want to count.

Have we graduated into adulthood in these years? I doubt it. I can only confess that though, from the outset, my orientation was moral and biblical, I have begun to realize that I am still a child in biblical faith. As we continue to face the Pentagon and the power of nuclear death that possesses (literally) all of us, the best of us despair of confronting it, the worst of us act in complicity with it. It becomes at once impossible and essential to act; we must perform an act of faith in the Lordship of Christ, whose death and resurrection have already defeated this power; we must issue a summons to this authority to fulfill its vocation to serve rather than to destroy humanity; we must live out a testament for anyone with eyes to see that the choice between God and mammon needs to be made in each heart, in each day.

Richard Mouw

A Christian Reformed Teacher

In 1978 I was a signer of "A Call to Faithfulness," joining Christians from a variety of groups in calling upon the United States to take specific steps toward halting the arms race. A number of people, including a few friends, expressed surprise and even dismay that I would affix my signature to such a document.

Had they known a little more about my past, these people would not have been so surprised that I harbored such sentiments. In the early 1960s, as a graduate student at a Canadian university, I was active in the leadership of the local chapter of the Combined University Campaign for Nuclear Disarmament, an affiliation that involved me in a number of "ban the bomb" activities. My views in this area of concern have changed very little since those days. But the truth of the matter is that, for many years, I did not aggressively express those views in any public forum. My decision to join the signers of the 1978 "Call" was a long overdue attempt to compensate for my years of virtual silence on the subject.

But I have still wondered why some people have expressed surprise over the fact that I harbor these convictions. My puzzlement was partially clarified by one of my friends, a rather "progressive" minister in the Calvinist denomination of which I am a member. He introduced the subject by assuring me that he regularly agrees with my stated views on political matters. Indeed, he insisted, he often endorses those views with great enthusiasm. "But this time, Richard—on this nuclear thing—this time you are too close to the Mennonites for my comfort!"

"Too close to the Mennonites." As a piece of historical or sociological analysis, my friend has a point. He and I are both committed Calvinists, Christians who accept the theology and social perspective of the Reformed branch of the Protestant Reformation. And we Calvinists are not pacifists. We believe that in this present age the state has been given the legitimate power of the sword. And we believe that the sword can be used for good purposes. We even believe—and this is what especially distinguishes us from many adherents to the historic "peace church" tradition—that Christians are permitted, even obligated on occasion, to support and participate in the state's exercise of the power of the sword. We believe that there can be—indeed, there have been—just wars in the course of sinful human history.

Calvinists, then, believe that Christian participation in acts of violence can be justified. Historically, this has been a sore point of contention between ourselves and Christian pacifists. And we Calvinists have been willing to argue long and passionately in defense of our perspective. As a result, we are not known for our eagerness to speak out against the use of bombs and guns and missiles. That is the kind of thing we expect to hear from Mennonites, Quakers— and perhaps from a few liberal Protestants and radical Catholics.

So, from an historical and sociological point of view, my friend's remark should not be surprising. But this is just to state the case in terms of expectations and stereotypes. It does not tell us anything about what Calvinists *ought* to be saying within the current dialogue about nuclear weapons.

My own impression is that orthodox Calvinists are afflicted with a "Mennophobia" of sorts. We want very much not to sound like radical Anabaptists. In our past debates with Christian pacifists, strong passions were fired on both sides. For our part, we have disagreed so strongly with the pacifists that we are disinclined to give them the satisfaction of conceding to them at any point. So if the Mennonites are known to talk in a certain manner, we will avoid sounding like them at all costs.

I believe that Calvinist Mennophobia is unhealthy. It is certainly not conducive to the kind of humility that is required of all Christians. And it can blind us to the truth. It can incapacitate us in our efforts to know the will of God. Indeed, it can cause us to be disobedient to the gospel.

It is time for Reformed Christians, and other Christians who are afflicted with a similar pathology, to cast aside their Mennophobic tendencies and take a careful look at the nuclear question. This is much needed, for at least four reasons.

First, we must acknowledge that all Christians, whether pacifist or non-pacifist, are committed to the task of peacemaking. Indeed, in the light of the importance of that task the whole debate over paci*fism* is somewhat of a misnomer. All Christians must be committed, without qualification, to peace, for they are servants of the Prince of Peace. The primary point of disagreement between so-called pacifists and non-pacifists ought to be viewed as the question of whether violent means are ever permissible elements in Christians' peace-directed strategies.

When I was participating in the 1969 "Vietnam Moratorium" in Washington, D.C., I spied, a half-block ahead of me in the line of march, a small sign bearing the words "A Calvinist for Peace." When I worked my way through the crowd to investigate this fascinating phenomenon, I found a male student from Westminster Theological Seminary in Philadelphia, who had thought it important to make the trip in order to raise a lonely voice from out of his theological tradition.

That small placard symbolizes for me the feebleness (but also the faithfulness) of the peace witness within the conservative Reformed environs which I call home. My colleague Nicholas Wolterstorff once remarked, after a visit to South Africa, that the Afrikaner Calvinists, when defending their racist practices, talk primarily about the need for order—with virtually no mention of justice. This observation can be carried a step further. Traditional Calvinists, even when they have been more "enlightened" in their political outlook than the white Reformed establishment of South Africa, have emphasized the Christian call to justice—with virtually no mention of the biblical concern for peace. This is a defect that cries out for repair.

Second, the time has come to test out in a very fundamental manner the contemporary applicability of the traditional just war doctrine to the current technological situation. I do not mean to suggest that we must abandon the traditional non-pacifist insistence that there *could be* or even that there *have been* just wars. Rather, we must ask whether there could actually be a just war today, given present levels of weapons development.

For example, traditional just war theory has insisted that in a just war there will be clear lines drawn between combatants and noncombatants as targets of military violence. Haven't we entered into an age in which the realistic application of this criterion is, at least for all practical purposes, impossible? Or take the traditional criterion of proportionality: according to which the use of military violence must be proportionate with respect to the intended, just, goals. The proliferation of weapons of mass destruction increases the likelihood that even a minor military effort could lead to far-reaching destruction.

The just war doctrine, properly understood, is not a weapon to be used in a battle with pacifists, nor is it a basis for reinforcing a war-mongering spirit. It is an instrument designed by Christians to test policies and actions out of a desire to serve the God of peace and justice. The doctrine most certainly ought not to serve to promote a callous spirit or to provide a facile argument for resorting to violence whenever a nation or individual is inclined to do so out of self-interest.

If the just war doctrine is, as I believe, correct, it is also dangerous. "We live in a sinful world, and it is sometimes necessary to do the lesser of two evils." True. But *we* live in a sinful world—and it is the recognition of the way in which sin has invaded even our innermost lives which is at the heart of a "realistic" Christian assessment of things. John Calvin put the general point well: "Man's disposition voluntarily so inclines to falsehood that he more quickly derives error from one word than truth from a wordy discourse."

The just war doctrine has been misused. It seems to *lend* itself to misuse. The violent spirit of Cain has embedded itself in our sinful souls to the extent that we—many of us at least—are prone to violence. And we are prone to facile justifications of our patterns of violence. The just war doctrine has served the devil well.

I must repeat: I believe it can also be an instrument for serving the Lord. But a sanctified use of the doctrine requires great caution and care. It must be used by Christians with an honest recognition that it always carries with it the tendency toward misuse. Those who insist on appealing to this doctrine need all of the help they can get if they are to do so with honesty and discernment. The Christian pacifist community, with its extreme pessimism and suspicion regarding the just war doctrine, can perform, then, an important service to those of us who believe that the doctrine has a legitimate use. Pacifists can help to keep us honest; they can force us continually to examine and reexamine our data, our assumptions, our assessments. If Mennonites did not exist, Calvinists would have to invent them. Thus the urgency of ridding the Christian world of Mennophobia.

Third, just war defenders have not always paid enough attention to the phenomenon of militarism. Many of us from non-pacifist groups took a stand against the war in Vietnam. And many of us were appalled by the elaborate pattern of deceit regarding that conflict which was perpetuated by the American military-political establishment. Yet our record since the withdrawal of U.S. troops from Indochina seems to indicate that we took that deceptive propaganda to be a mere temporary aberration. But was it?

The Scriptures clearly warn against idolatry. And the Bible is very clear about the fact that idolatry can take a corporate, even political or military, shape. Nations exhibit an empirically observable tendency to take pride in military might, in their power to destroy enemies. Why have Christians, especially just war Christians, been so silent about this tendency?

Finally, Reformed Christians must think long and hard about how their confession concerning God's good creation bears on their witness in a nuclear age. There is, I think, an irony to be noted here. In Calvinist circles—certainly in those circles which adhere to the "Christ-transforming-culture" perspective—there is much talk about creation. "Redemption is the restoration of the original creation." "Sinful culture is a distortion of a created good." "God has not cancelled his creational norms."

Mennonites, on the other hand, are thought of as being weak on creation. They see the present order, not as a distorted, but essentially good, creation, but as an essentially evil order that is heading for destruction. They are skeptical of talk about creational norms. Their Jesus—or so the rumor goes—is not a restorer of that which God originally called good; he is a thoroughgoing confrontationalist, a radical opponent of all that is in the world.

That is the way the contrast is often set up—from the Calvinist side. Now here is the irony: when it comes to the nuclear issue, the Mennonites talk creation while the Calvinists talk fall. The Mennonites want to till the garden; they want to preserve the world. They do not want to be responsible for the destruction of created reality. And what do we hear from the Calvinists? "We live in a fallen world." "We are, after all, *sinners!*"

Every day the United States produces materials for three nuclear bombs. The present nuclear stockpile of the American government could destroy the present world population twelve times over. What does the Reformed confession concerning creation say about this situation? The issue here is not pacifism. The question is

133

whether we are willing to examine the current military-technological situation in the light of cherished notions of stewardship and creation and cultural mandate.

I am pleased to be close to the Mennonites on the nuclear question. I disavow Mennophobia, and I call for a similar action on the part of my fellow just war theorists. And I do so in the name of all that is good and true and worthy of acceptance in my own Reformed tradition.

Andre Gingerich

A Draft Resister

While working with the Sojourners housing ministry under the auspices of the voluntary service program of the Mennonite Board of Missions, Andre Gingerich was interviewed for Sojourners *magazine by Danny Collum on his decision to refuse to register for the draft.*

Danny Collum: As a Mennonite, you could have fairly easily chosen the conscientious objection option. How did you make the decision instead to refuse to register for the draft?

Andre Gingerich: I was brought up with a strong sense that the Christian life is a life of discipleship, and that pacifism is very central to that. Respect for the sacredness of life is very important, and the taking of life is contradictory to the Christian life.

In the summer of 1979, there was a lot of talk of reviving the draft. I was part of a mock draft board at a local church. I had just graduated from high school.

At that point it was assumed that the participants took the role of registrants trying to defend our position as conscientious objectors. I went through that in this mock board. But somewhere in the back of my mind, I was thinking there seemed to be a contradiction between us trying to find our special exemption, while all those other people out there would still be drafted and were considered beyond our concern.

As I started thinking more and more about the draft issue, a crucial part of my decision was working through it with other people. I kept in close communication with one friend in particular, named Luke, who was up in New York attending school while I was in college in Pennsylvania. We decided not to register and were working through the questions together.

I had some feelings that the Mennonites too often were concerned about maintaining their own personal consistency and morality and were not really very concerned about what was going on in a broader sense. If there was a war going on, they wanted to make sure they weren't participating, but weren't doing too much to make sure the war wasn't happening.

My ideas solidified when I was reading something from the National Resistance Committee, which is a secular group trying to build a coalition of resisters. It pointed out that the government has established conscientious objector status to further the aims of the conscription process, by giving those who are most likely to oppose conscription special exemption. By working within the conscription system, you're giving that system the political and moral authority to draft others.

I realized that registration is a very crucial part of the whole process, and that one's opposition to war should not start at the actual point of killing nor at the point of induction. Our whole life has to be a life of resistance to the hate and murder that war is about. And at that point I decided that I couldn't participate in registration.

I think we have to be concerned about a whole lot more than just our own consistency, and I think as a Christian I need to be opposing war before it starts, so to speak. I need to stand clear in my opposition, not just to my own fighting but for other people trying to solve conflict in that kind of way. So, not registering has a lot of political significance in that when people refuse to register, it makes the whole war process very difficult from the beginning. In not registering, there's a lot of opportunity to generate and stimulate thinking and to challenge people to look at their own position, and there's a lot of opportunity to start mobilizing opposition.

Collum: Once you decided to refuse registration, what was the process in your thinking to decide to do that publicly?

Gingerich: From the very beginning, I felt that I at least wanted to discuss it with my family and friends, and I was public in that arena. I also felt that this was an issue that the Mennonite church should deal with, and so Luke and I went through quite a process in our home congregation.

As we were doing that, we went to a Mobilization for Survival training seminar in Philadelphia. We came back feeling the urgency of the whole military buildup, especially the nuclear threat, and the need for people to come out strongly against what's happening. We started talking to other people in our community and organized a presence at the post office during the first two weeks of draft registration. I think there was probably more of a witness to the Mennonites in our community than to anybody else. One of the best things that happened there was that we called up people, Mennonites, and said, "Can you come down to the post office and join us?" as if we expected that they would.

Last summer we established a network of, and started a newsletter for, Mennonite non-registrants. Those non-registrants decided we wanted to address the broader church.

Every two years, the Mennonite church has a gathering for all its members, generally two to three thousand; last summer it also had a youth convention of about two thousand with it. We stood up, five of us, and made a statement, asking for the church's support in the months ahead, because we were anticipating some prosecution. Especially during the grace period, as the government began to put pressure on people to register, I felt it was important that people stand up and be very vocal about their position. In that way others who were considering that position wouldn't be badgered into making a decision on the basis of fear because they felt they were alone. That's when I started becoming even more public. So when the opportunity came along for me to go on the *Today Show,* I decided to do that too.

Collum: Could you say more about the response you've gotten from your home church and your immediate family?

Gingerich: My family and friends have been very supportive. They wanted to make sure, of course, that I was choosing what I wanted to do, because one of the important things about making that kind of decision is that you have to grapple with the possible consequences.

The home congregation response was very interesting. Luke and I had written up a statement outlining three different reasons for taking our position. One Sunday morning, instead of breaking up into Sunday School, the whole congregation stayed together, and we presented this paper and had a period of discussion. We got several different kinds of responses.

Some were very supportive. But some of the people who had done alternative service during World War II felt very threatened. They felt that we were negating what they had done, or accusing them of taking a position without integrity. And they really had to get that off their shoulders.

The Mennonite church has become, like a lot of churches,

very institutionalized, and we're working hard at becoming part of the mainstream of American life—quite affluent in a lot of ways. Some of our leading members are very prestigious in the community, reputable businessmen and doctors, and there was a lot of concern expressed that what we were doing was going to cause a bad name for the Mennonite church.

Then there was a general feeling that, "You're being negative. . . . Instead of just spending time in jail and rotting away, you should be making a positive contribution to society."

One of the comical moments was when somebody stood up in front and said, "Now, I'm having a little difficult time understanding what all these comments about being negative are about. I'm wondering if we would have the same reaction if a girl would say no in the back of a Chevy van." The whole congregation roared and broke through it and put it in perspective.

We had three or four sessions with the congregation before they took any kind of position. There were some really touching moments, too. One person in his sixties, whose son had been part of Sojourners when you were in Chicago, stood up and in a quiet voice said, "I've got several sons. One of them joined a Christian group in Chicago and has been working for peace. One of them went to Vietnam, and he's a killer. And I support these young men wholeheartedly. I'd make my house available to them. Anything that's mine is theirs." It was a real moving kind of thing for me to feel that kind of support.

It's much more acceptable now in the Mennonite church not to register than it was back during the Vietnam War. Yet I think people like those at the big Mennonite gathering in the summer are sort of uneasy about the whole thing. They support us, but when you start drawing out the implications, it makes people uncomfortable. But last summer, after the five of us stood up and read the statement and then walked away from the podium, we got a standing ovation, which we were not at all expecting.

Collum: What, if any, response have you received from the government about your refusing to register?

Gingerich: I've gotten none. I didn't write the Selective Service a letter. It seems that most people who did got responses.

I felt that the people I wanted to address, first of all, were the people in the Mennonite church, and eighteen-year-olds now facing this decision, and the public in general—people who are having questions about the wisdom of our national and military policies. I really placed hope in people responding and thinking about what I was trying to say. I guess I didn't put that much hope in the director of Selective Service or the president.

Collum: What's happening with the young men who did write the Selective Service?

Gingerich: First they got letters from the Selective Service saying that if they didn't register they'd be turned over to the Justice Department. A lot of them responded by saying they still wouldn't register. Then their names were turned over to the Justice Department, and since then there have been several FBI visits. At one point when Reagan was still unclear on his position, it seemed that indictments were actually going to come down. But then Reagan stopped that at the last moment because he hadn't really taken a formal position.

So at this point, I think the government is preparing its case on some individuals. And I think there will probably be prosecution in the next two or three months, probably after school's out. The government's been very wise about its threats. The first big registration period was in the summer of 1980. And the next one came over Christmas vacation, and ever since then it's been a continuous registration, so that it's been much more difficult to mobilize people.

Collum: Has the government gone after people whom they found out about through the media? Are they trying to encourage informers?

Gingerich: They keep saying they're getting a lot of names from mothers whose sons registered who don't think it's fair that others didn't. From my experience, that's not been the case. They have obtained some mass mailing lists, and they've sent, in certain states, postcards to everybody of registration age, saying they're supposed to register. Some non-registrants who had received them were under the impression that they had been singled out, but they hadn't.

Collum: The estimates are that there are about 800,000 to a million resisters.

Gingerich: That has changed some. Now, after Reagan's grace period, the Selective Service figure is 535,000. Apparently, and I wouldn't doubt this, there were a good number of people who didn't know. And there was also probably a large number of people who decided not to register, but weren't strong in their position, and with some pressure and threats decided to register after all. But even so, 535,000 is a very substantial number of non-registrants.

Collum: It's obvious that there is a resistance movement developing, with support groups of resisters. How is that growing?

Gingerich: My main experience in a movement has been in the Mennonite church and in colleges. The campuses that I'm most familiar with have groups of ten or fifteen non-registrants meeting once a week and keeping in touch, talking about their feelings, their fears. It's very supportive and important, and it keeps the position alive.

There have been several gatherings. The Mennonite resisters all got together in February of 1981 in Kansas. And this January again we had a weekend. The National Resistance Committee organized gatherings in New York, Chicago, and San Francisco not too long ago, just to keep people tied together and also to find strategies in terms of how non-registrants can be supported legally in their position.

Also we get out, for example, in the high schools and present our position there. Young men are being required to register before they even graduate from high school. And it's really important that people know what their options are and have thought it through.

So, I think a movement is beginning to get organized. There are clearly large numbers of non-registrants. And that's exciting.

Collum: Among the resisters that you come in contact with, what's the general spirit, what are the expectations, how's the morale?

Gingerich: Well, I think we all were a little naive getting into this whole thing. We expected a lot of quick action, a lot of excitement. I remember that first summer, we thought the prosecution would begin in four or five months. And it turned out that the Supreme Court didn't even decide if the draft was constitutional for a year and a half or so.

For a lot of us, there were periods where our resistance was our identity. In my life, for a while, that was the only thing I was— a non-registrant. That's what I breathed, and talked—it was everything. For most of us now, it's a very important part of who we are, but we've decided that life moves on.

I don't think there's a great deal of anxiety. As more and more people come out in support of non-registrants or come out in opposition to the military buildup and the nuclear arms race, that strengthens us and keeps our spirits up. For some of the individuals who were most likely to face prosecution, there have been real rough times. But again, I think the thing that is so crucial is that continued display of support from others.

I had a lot of fear and anxiety in the beginning. I spent a lot of time thinking about the possibility of jail. I went ahead and chose not to register, but I hadn't settled anything about how I felt about the possibility of jail. It was frightening just to imagine the isolation that that would bring.

When Luke and I came back that summer and got the presence at the post office going, some folks continued to meet after that and started a group called Christians for Peace. One of the things that was really strengthening for me and helped free me to move on was when about thirty people from that group wrote a letter to the director of the Selective Service saying that they advocate non-registration and were in total support of those who didn't register. They said they recognized that advocating non-registration is a felony—just like refusing to register—and though they probably wouldn't be prosecuted, they said they were willing to start taking the same kinds of risks in their lives that we were taking. These were older folks—members of the college faculty, businessmen, a doctor—and there was a real commitment. I knew that I wasn't alone, that if things started happening to me, other people were going to help share the cost and the weight of it.

Collum: Do you still feel any fear?

Gingerich: It comes and goes. But there are many times when I feel lots of support, and lots of love. One of the most moving experiences was at the worship service at Sojourners, just after the grace period ended. I felt strong support and love in a way that I've never felt before. Maybe that's what's meant by the love of Christ. I think of the passage that says nothing can separate us from the love of Christ. If I ever were to face jail, such experiences would help carry me through.

I've tried to familiarize myself with what a jail setting is like. We're often most afraid of things we don't know about. So I've had some important conversations with people who spent time in jail during the Vietnam War years. It's been a good thing to see that they've come out, many times even stronger; and at the least they've survived.

A lot of times I've thought, why, at nineteen, would I want to spend time in jail? I really don't want to. But I think we need to take that step of faithfulness sometimes before we have everything worked out, and before we deal with the issue of expectation or our own strength. I think sometimes we just need to step forward. There is a rich legacy of those who have gone before; and jail, I think, has served as a place to really solidify and strengthen people in their faith.

Collum: What connection do you see between your work in housing here in Washington and your stance on draft registration?

Gingerich: I'm working with the housing ministry of Sojourners community, with the Southern Columbia Heights Tenants Union. Our work is with low-income tenants in northwest Washington, helping them to organize and bring their landlords to accountability, to get the basics of housing—water, heat, decent and affordable housing.

The broader concern is that poor people find ways to take control of what's happening in their lives, so that they're not always at the mercy of the real estate agents, or the landlords, or the developers. In our neighborhood, the issues of displacement and gentrification are very much alive, and they're a real threat to the lives of the people.

When people are refused the basics of decent housing, when such a situation of injustice exists, it generates violence and hate and distrust. On a national or global level, when one or more countries consume inordinate percentages of natural resources, whether or not they're actually fighting and killing, when that setting of injustice exists, they're actually in a continual state of war. And I guess I'm inclined to believe that if we're really serious about trying to find peace, then we have to become much more serious about establishing justice.

Collum: Do you feel that you're able to communicate that you're resisting the draft because of your faith?

Gingerich: I think people have a tendency to see anybody who's resisting as a wild-eyed leftover from the '60s. When I begin to express some of my religious convictions, sometimes it stops people short. Most people in our country claim some kind of religious belief, so, in a sense, it hits them on their home turf. And it causes people to re-examine their beliefs.

I try to figure out who my audience is and speak in terms that they understand. I always try to get the value of human life and respect and care and love across, whether or not I use religious language.

The example of Christ shows that people are more important than institutions and law and custom—he healed on the sabbath, he associated with the publicans and the prostitutes, and he made people more important than the national interests. He preached love for enemies, and that was quite a threat to the people of his time, as it's still a threat now.

There's something about that concern and deep caring for people and life which is so fundamental and yet so radical; and when I present my position in those terms people have to respond to it. It's different than presenting some kind of ideology or plan for how the world's going to change. Just a concern for human life: I'm taking this position because I see registering and participating in the military as a dehumanization, as a refusal of the element of God in other people.

Collum: Do you see a connection between the government asking you to sign up for the army and the threat of nuclear war that many people are getting concerned about now?

Gingerich: Most definitely. For many years we've made this nice, neat distinction between conventional war and nuclear war. It just can't be made anymore. Any move toward conventional war at this point is, in real terms, a move toward nuclear war.

The urgency of nuclear war is one of the things that caused me to take seriously the draft issue. It makes me more willing to take the risk. The government is requiring an act of obedience which primes the nation for readiness for nuclear war. It escalates the level of violence in our society.

Dietrich Bonhoeffer said that only they who believe obey, and they who obey believe. When people take that first step of obedience to the government, it becomes easier to believe the need for nuclear weapons, for a strong military, and for the possibility of fighting nuclear war.

The latest draft emerged after the Soviet invasion of Afghanistan. One image that came to my mind was of two gang leaders getting their troops together to flex their muscle. Part of that process is preparing the members of the gang for the fight that could come up. I just didn't want to be part of that gang.

Mary Evelyn Jegen

A Notre Dame Sister

During the summer between my junior and senior years of high school, when I was working for my father in the family florist shop, the United States dropped the atomic bombs on Hiroshima and Nagasaki. My father said simply that the war would soon be over. He was correct. A few days later we closed early, went to the Cathedral to say a prayer, and stopped at the Tribune Tower to buy a special issue of the *Chicago Tribune,* which my father said would be a historic issue.

Yet the war that hardly broke the routine of a teenager in Chicago was, as anthropologist Margaret Mead noted, the dividing line not between two generations but between two civilizations. What happened in World War II radically changed the inner universe of our consciousness, of our sensibilities, of our moral powers—even though there is now an entire generation that cannot remember Hiroshima. We are in a state of shock, numbed by an event beyond our imagination and somehow still beyond our compassion. We are sick, and we do not know it. Can we be cured?

Hiroshima brought to a climax a way of relating to people not as members of the same human family but as enemies to be brought to unconditional surrender by a total victory. The psychology of total victory, of unconditional surrender, antedates the Bomb, of course, but use of the Bomb "to bring an end to the war" translated the attitude into an act of a new kind. The political-military establishment has told us we must be willing and able to kill children in their classrooms, old people in their beds, mothers and fathers in their homes and at work, to defend our way of life, our honor.

In placing such a high priority on defense through nuclear deterrence, we have forced millions of our people to turn their vital energies day in, day out, year in, year out, to the manufacture of life-destroying rather than life-enhancing "goods," and those people have had to pay a penalty. Whether we turn out a painting that hangs in the Metropolitan Museum or a freshly painted room, whether we make a Supreme Court decision or an apple pie, whether we design a nuclear-powered missile or one of its components, what we make becomes an extension of ourselves. In making something, we are at the same time making ourselves, changing ourselves, growing or diminishing. All life-enhancing works can, and do, bring us into communion: such works as a meal, a song, a parade, the telephone, a good piece of legislation. Life-destroying works drive us apart through the fear, suspicion, and anxiety they create: such works as slings, arrows, swords, spears, guns, bombs, missiles.

We are now at a hinge of history. A persistent, rugged common sense tells us that our way of life, our honor, cannot survive another holocaust. For as Father Dick McSorley, S.J., has cautioned, although Soviet weapons can destroy our bodies, our willingness to use nuclear weapons can destroy our souls. Our survival depends on our cure, on whether we are given the insight to see that defense could be better provided by tools and works of communion than by the tools and works of alienation. Our salvation depends on our obedience to God's command to keep the Sabbath holy, to take time out to contemplate the works of our hands, to pay attention to what we have done, to take care, to be full of care, lest we destroy the fragile ecosystem that we call home. If we want to keep the planet for the family, we will have to treat it, and one another, with much greater gentleness and respect.

I find great hope in the young who are claiming their dignity by asserting their right to refuse to kill, and I find enormous comfort in the fact that the Church is supporting these conscientious objectors—certainly by an increasingly clear and developed pastoral theology, and less evenly by adequate pastoral counseling and support. The genius of love at work springs from such a recognition of human dignity, of each person as infinitely precious, with a meaning immeasurable by any of the norms we use for assessing the worth or value of economic goods.

Yesterday, coming home on a crowded airline flight, my attention was captured by a young mother and her baby boy. How fragile, how absolutely dependent for survival he was, and how marvelous. Studying him, thinking about his promise and his hope for the future, I could not escape the fact that God became just like him. As always, I was uncomfortable with the thought, as I am uncomfortable with all the other truths of my faith that hang on this central mystery of God's love saving us from inside our own flesh and bone, nerve and muscle, mind and heart.

How can I comprehend such grace? Yet if we are to be saved from the consequences of permitting the nuclear competition that is driving us to destruction, it will be as a consequence of grace, the gift to accept ourselves as we truly are: fragile, weak, disordered—yet loved and loving, a little less than the angels, entrusted with each other's lives. How delicate is the balance on which our survival depends!

Perhaps we are at last coming to see that our most deadly enemy is fear. We are frightened almost to death by our ingenious hostility, which has wired the earth for genocide. We cannot conquer that enemy; we can only be delivered from it by love in the form of trust. Gandhi knew that the only safe way to overcome an enemy is to make of the enemy a friend. Are we capable of receiving the gift on which our cure depends? We are schooled to believe that we cannot trust the Soviets, and yet, if we are honest, we admit that we cannot even trust ourselves.

Only you, Lord, can save us from ourselves. It is not the technology that threatens us. It is not the Soviet Union. It is the killer in our own hearts, in the hearts of Christians, in *my* heart, which stands in the way of your spirit filling the earth, making it safe and nurturing.

Save us from ourselves, Lord. Stay with us while you tutor us in the politics of love.

Daniel Berrigan

A Poet and Priest

On September 9, 1980, Father Daniel Berrigan and seven others were involved in a civil disobedience action at a General Electric plant in King of Prussia, Pennsylvania, which makes parts for the Mark 12A nuclear missile. They were convicted on eight of thirteen counts at their trial in Norristown, Pennsylvania, in March, 1981, during which they acted as their own attorneys. All the defendants are out of jail and appealing their convictions. Following is Daniel Berrigan's response to direct examination by Sister Anne Montgomery at their trial.

Anne Montgomery: Father Berrigan, I'd like to ask you a simple question: Why did you do what you did?

Daniel Berrigan: I would like to answer that question as simply as I can. It brings up immediately words that have been used again and again in the courtroom—like conscience, justification. The question takes me back to those years when my conscience was being formed, back to a family that was poor, and to a father and mother who taught, quite simply, by living what they taught. And if I could put their message very shortly, it would go something like this:

In a thousand ways they showed that you do what is right because it is right, that your conscience is a matter between you and God, that nobody owns you.

If I have a precious memory of my mother and father that lasts to this day, it is simply that they lived as though nobody owned them. They cheated no one. They worked hard for a living.

They were poor; and, perhaps most precious of all, they shared what they had. And that was enough, because in the life of a young child, the first steps of conscience are as important as the first steps of one's feet. They set the direction where life will go.

And I feel that direction was set for my brothers and myself.

There is a direct line between the way my parents turned our steps and this action. That is no crooked line.

That was the first influence. The second one has to do with my religious order. When I was eighteen I left home for the Jesuit order. I reflect that I am sixty years old, and I have never been anything but a Jesuit, a Jesuit priest, in my whole life.

We have Jesuits throughout Latin America today, my own brothers, who are in prison, who have been under torture; many of them have been murdered.

On the walls of our religious communities both here and in Latin America are photos of murdered priests, priests who have been imprisoned, priests under torture, priests who stood somewhere because they believed in something. Those faces haunt my days. And I ask myself how I can be wishy-washy in face of such example, example of my own lifetime, my own age.

This is a powerful thing, to be in a common bond of vows with people who have given their lives because they did not believe in mass murder, because such crimes could not go on in their name.

Dear friends of the jury, you have been called the conscience of the community. Each of us eight comes from a community. I don't mean just a biological family. I mean that every one of us has brothers and sisters with whom we live, with whom we pray, with whom we offer the Eucharist, with whom we share income, and in some cases, the care of children. Our conscience, in other words, comes from somewhere. We have not come from outer space or from chaos or from madhouses to King of Prussia.

We have come from years of prayer, years of life together, years of testing—testing of who we are in the church and in the world. We would like to speak to you, each of us in a different way, about our communities; because, you see, it is our conviction that nobody in the world can form his or her conscience alone.

Now, perhaps I don't even have to dwell on that. Most of you who have children know the importance of others—not just parents, but friends, relatives, those who are loved and who love, in helping us come to understand who we are.

What are we to do in bad times? I am trying to say that we come as a community of conscience before your community of conscience to ask you: Are our consciences to act differently than yours in regard to the lives and deaths of children? A very simple question, but one that cuts to the bone.

We would like you to see that we come from where you come. We come from churches. We come from neighborhoods. We come from years of work.

We come from America. And we come to this, a trial, of conscience and motive. And the statement of conscience we would like to present to you is this.

We could not not do this. We could not not do this! We were pushed to this by all our lives. Do you see what I mean? All our lives.

I would speak about myself, the others will speak for themselves. When I say I could not not do this, I mean, among other things, that with every cowardly bone in my body I wished I hadn't had to enter the GE plant. I wish I hadn't had to do it. And that has been true every time I have been arrested, all those years. My stomach turns over. I feel sick. I feel afraid. I don't want to go through this again.

I hate jail. I don't do well there physically. But I cannot not go on, because I have learned that we must not kill if we are Christians. I have learned that children, above all, are threatened by these weapons. I have read that Christ our Lord underwent death rather than inflict it. And I am supposed to be a disciple. All kinds of things like that. The push, the push of conscience is a terrible thing.

So at some point your cowardly bones get moving, and you say, "Here it goes again," and you do it. And you have a certain peace because you did it, as I do this morning in speaking with you.

That phrase about not being able not to do something, maybe it is a little clumsy. But for those who raise children, who go to work every day, who must make decisions in their families, I think there is a certain knowledge of what I am trying to say. Children at times must be disciplined. We would rather not do it.

There are choices on jobs about honesty. There are things to be gained if we are dishonest. And it is hard not to be.

Yet one remains honest because one has a sense, "Well, if I cheat, I'm really giving over my humanity, my conscience." Then we think of these horrible Mark 12A missiles, something in us says, "We cannot live with such crimes." Or, our consciences turn in another direction. And by a thousand pressures, a thousand silences, people can begin to say to themselves, "We can live with that. We can live with that. We know it's there. We know what it is

149

for. We know that many thousands will die if only one of these is exploded."

And yet we act like those employees, guards, experts we heard speak here; they close their eyes, close their hearts, close their briefcases, take their paycheck—and go home. It's called living with death. And it puts us to death before the missile falls.

We believe, according to the law, the law of the state of Pennsylvania, that we were justified in saying, "We cannot live with that"; justified in saying it publicly, saying it dramatically, saying it with blood and hammers, as you have heard; because that weapon, the hundreds and hundreds more being produced in our country, are the greatest evil conceivable on this earth.

There is no evil to compare with that. Multiply murder. Multiply desolation. The mind boggles.

So we went into that death factory, and in a modest, self-contained, careful way we put a few dents in two missiles, awaited arrest, came willingly into court to talk to you. We believe with all our hearts that our action was justified.

Montgomery: You mentioned work. Could you say something about how your work in the cancer hospital in New York influenced your decision?

Berrigan: Sure. I wouldn't want the jury to get the impression we are always going around banging on nose cones. We also earn a living. I have been doing, among other things, a kind of service to the dying for about three years now in New York. And I would like to speak shortly about that, because I come to you from an experience of death—not just any death, but the death of the poor, death by cancer.

I don't know whether you have ever smelled cancer. Cancer of the nose, cancer of the face, which is the most terrible to look upon and to smell, cancer of the brain, cancer of the lungs: We see it all, smell it all, hold it all in our arms.

This is not just a lecture on cancer. It is a lecture on those Mark 12A missiles, which make cancer the destiny of humanity, as is amply shown. This is another aspect of our justification.

We know now that in Hiroshima and Nagasaki, those who did not die at the flash point are still dying of cancer. Nuclear weapons carry a universal plague of cancer. As the Book of Revelation implies, after one of these missiles is launched, the living will envy the dead.

I could not understand cancer until I was arrested at the Pentagon, because there I smelled death by cancer, in my very soul. I smelled the death of everyone, everyone, across the board: black, brown, red, all of us, death by cancer.

So I talk to the dying. I take a chance on the dying, those that are still able to talk. And I say, "Do you know where my friends and I go from here?" Some of the patients know; and some of them don't. Some had read of our act in the papers. Some hadn't. I would talk about what I can only call the politics of cancer. The service the dying were rendering me was this: With their last days, their last breath, they helped me understand why I had to continue this struggle; because in them I was seeing up close the fate of everyone, and especially the children.

I have seen children dying of cancer. And we will see more and more of that as these bombs are built.

Justification and conscience. Could I mention briefly also that for two semesters I have been teaching at a college in the South Bronx, a college for poor people? It's a unique place, because only poor people who cannot pay are admitted. We have some one thousand students who are finishing degrees. You have undoubtedly seen pictures of the South Bronx; Carter and President Reagan have visited there. It's a required campaign stop by now; and when pictures appear one thinks of a president stepping on the moon, a lunar landscape, a landscape of utter desolation and misery and poverty and neglect.

This is also to our point of justification, because I have been led to ask, "Why are people condemned to live this way in a wealthy country?" Where is the money going? Why is there a culture of poverty? Why are people born into it? Why do they live outside the economy, never have a job, have no future, live and die that way, hundreds of thousands in the South Bronx?

I don't know what to call our college. It is like a center for survivors. I look at the faces of these marvelous people, my students. And I think with sorrow in my heart that for every one who sits in that room, twenty have died on the way, or are in prison or are on drugs or are suicides, have given up.

And I was led to ask, "Why must this be?" So the cancer hospital and the college lead me to the Pentagon. I discussed freely in class, why are we so poor? Where is the money? General Electric costs the poor three million dollars a day, not for housing, not for schooling, not for neighborhood rehabilitation, not for medical care—for Mark 12A; three million dollars a day stolen from the poor. A larceny of worldwide proportions. This is our justification. We could not be indefinitely silent.

The hospital, the college, and the Pentagon, this is the circuit of my life.

In each of these places I learn more about the other two. At the Pentagon I understand why cancer will befall everyone, and why so many are destitute now. Among the poor, I understand why the poor die in such numbers of cancer. And at the hospital I smell the death that is planned for all.

Montgomery: Getting to the King of Prussia action itself, would you describe something of the preparation for it?

Berrigan: I'm sure, dear friends, that others will speak of the great import to us of the spiritual life, our lives in God. I want to tell you a little about the immediate days preceding this action; indeed, about days that have preceded every arrest we have undergone.

We have never taken actions such as these, perilous, crucial, difficult as they are, without the most careful preparation of our hearts, our motivation, our common sense, our sense of one another. We have never admitted any person to our groups whom we could not trust to be nonviolent under pressure of crises.

This is simply a rule of our lives; we don't go from the street to do something like the King of Prussia action. We go from prayer. We go from reflection. We go from worship, always. And since we realized that this action was perhaps the most difficult of all our lives, we spent more time in prayer this time than before.

We passed three days together in a country place. We prayed, and read the Bible, and shared our fears, shared our second and third thoughts.

And in time we drew closer. We were able to say, "Yes. We can do this. We can take the consequences. We can undergo whatever is required." All of that.

During those days we sweated out the question of families and children—the question of a long separation if we were convicted and jailed.

I talked openly with Jesuit friends and superiors. They respected my conscience and said, "Do what you are called to."

That was the immediate preparation. And what it issued in was a sense that, with great peacefulness, with calm of spirit, even though with a butterfly in our being, we could go ahead. And so we did.

This enters into my understanding of conscience and justification, a towering question, which has faced so many good people in history, in difficult times, now, in the time of the bomb. What helps people? What helps people understand who they are in the world, who they are in their families, who they are with their children, with their work? What helps?

That was a haunting question for me. Will this action be helpful? Legally, we could say that this was our effort to put the question of justification. Will our action help? Will people understand that this "lesser evil," done to this so-called "property," was helping turn things around in the church, in the nation?

Will the action help us be more reflective, about life and death and children and children and all life?

We have spent years and years of our adult lives keeping the law. We have tried everything, every access, every means to get to public authorities within the law. We come from within the law, from within.

We are deeply respectful of a law that is in favor of human life. And as we know, at least some of our laws are. We are very respectful of those laws. We want you to know that.

Years and years we spent writing letters, trying to talk to authorities, vigiling in public places, holding candles at night, holding placards by day, trying, trying, fasting, trying to clarify things to ourselves as we were trying to speak to others; all of that within the law, years of it.

And then I had to say, I could not not break the law and remain human. That was what was in jeopardy: what I call my conscience, my humanity, that which is recognizable to children, to friends, to good people, when we say, "There is someone I can trust and love, someone who will not betray."

We spent years within the law, trying to be that kind of person, a non-betrayer.

Then we found we couldn't. And if we kept forever on this side of the line, we would die within, ourselves. We couldn't look in the mirror, couldn't face those we love, had no Christian message in the world, nothing to say if we went on that way.

I might just as well wander off and go the way pointed to by a low-grade American case of despair: getting used to the way things are. That is what I mean by dying. That is what we have to oppose. I speak for myself.

The Jesuit order accepted me as a member. The Catholic Church ordained me as a priest. I took all that with great seriousness. I still do, with all my heart. And then Vietnam came along, and then the nukes came along. And I had to continue to ask myself at prayer, with my friends, with my family, with all kinds of people, with my own soul, "Do you have anything to say today?" I mean, beyond a lot of prattling religious talk.

Do you have anything to say about life today, about the lives of people today? Do you have a word, a word of hope to offer, a Christian word? That's a very important question for anyone who takes being a priest, being a Christian, being a human being seriously, "Do you have anything to offer human life today?"

It is a terribly difficult question for me. And I am not at all sure that I do have something to offer. But I did want to say this. I am quite certain that I had September 9th, 1980, to say.

And I will never deny, whether here or in jail, to my family, or friends, or to the Russians, or the Chinese, or anyone in the world, I will never deny what I did.

More than that. Our act is all I have to say. The only message I have to the world is: We are not allowed to kill innocent people. We are not allowed to be complicit in murder. We are not allowed to be silent while preparations for mass murder proceed in our name, with our money, secretly.

I have nothing else to say in the world. At other times one could talk about family life and divorce and birth control and abortion and many other questions. But this Mark 12A is here. And it renders all other questions null and void. Nothing, nothing can be settled until this is settled. Or this will settle us, once and for all.

It's terrible for me to live in a time where I have nothing to say to human beings except, "Stop killing." There are other beautiful things that I would love to be saying to people. There are other projects I could be very helpful at. And I can't do them. I cannot.

Because everything is endangered. Everything is up for grabs. Ours is a kind of primitive situation, even though we would call ourselves sophisticated. Our plight is very primitive from a Christian point of view. We are back where we started. Thou shall not kill; we are not allowed to kill. Everything today comes down to that—everything.

I thank you with all my heart for listening.

Contributors

Janet Aldridge works with the educationally handicapped in Santa Clara, California.

Robert Aldridge served as a design engineer for Lockheed Missiles and Space Company for sixteen years, working on the Polaris, Poseidon, and Trident missile systems. He is the author of *First Strike* (South End Press, 1982) and *The Counterforce Syndrome: A Guide to U.S. Nuclear Weapons and Strategic Doctrine* (Transnational Institute, 1978).

Richard Barnet is a senior fellow at the Institute for Policy Studies in Washington, D.C. He is the author of several books, including *The Lean Years* (Simon and Schuster, 1980) and *Real Security: Restoring American Power in a Dangerous Decade* (Simon and Schuster, 1981). He is a contributing editor for *Sojourners* magazine.

Daniel Berrigan is a Jesuit priest, a poet, a peace activist, and the author of many books, including most recently *Portraits* (Crossroad, 1982) and *Prison Poems* (Unicorn Press, 1982). He is a contributing editor for *Sojourners* magazine.

Joan Chittister is prioress of the Benedictine Sisters of Erie, Pennsylvania. She is past president and current member of the Leadership Conference of Women Religious, and a contributing editor for *Sojourners* magazine.

James Douglass is a member of Ground Zero, a resistance community in Bangor, Washington, and the author of *The Nonviolent Cross* (Macmillan Publishing Company, 1966), *Lightning East to West* (Sunburst Press, 1980) and *Resistance and Contemplation* (Doubleday, 1971).

Andre Gingerich is a history major at Swarthmore College in Swarthmore, Pennsylvania.

Billy Graham is an evangelist, and the author of several books.

Thomas Gumbleton is auxiliary bishop of Detroit, Michigan, and the president of Pax Christi, U.S.A.

Vincent Harding is professor of religion and social transformation at Iliff School of Religion in Denver, Colorado, and the author, most recently, of *There Is a River* (Harcourt, Brace, Jovanovich, 1981).

Raymond Hunthausen is archbishop of Seattle, Washington.

Mary Evelyn Jegen is a Sister of Notre Dame of Namur and the former national coordinator of Pax Christi, U.S.A.

Bill Kellermann is a Methodist pastor in Detroit, a member of the Detroit peace community, and a contributing editor for *Sojourners* magazine.

Mary Lou Kownacki is a member of the Benedictine Sisters of Erie, Pennsylvania. She is a founder and national coordinator of Benedictines for Peace and the founder of Pax Center.

Leroy Matthiesen is bishop of Amarillo, Texas.

Elizabeth McAlister is a longtime peace activist and member of Jonah House, a Christian resistance community in Baltimore, Maryland.

Virginia Ramey Mollenkott is professor of English at William Paterson College in Wayne, New Jersey, and the author, most recently, of *Biblical Imagery of God as Female* (Crossroad, 1983) and, with Catherine Barry, of *Views from the Intersection* (Crossroad, 1983).

Richard Mouw is professor of philosophy at Calvin College in Grand Rapids, Michigan. He is the author of *Political Evangelism* (Eerdmans, 1973), *Politics and the Biblical Drama* (Eerdmans, 1976), and *Call to Holy Worldliness* (Fortress Press, 1980).

John Perkins is the president emeritus and minister-at-large of Voice of Calvary Ministries and the author of *With Justice for All* (Regal, 1982).

Molly Rush is director of the Thomas Merton Center in Pittsburgh, Pennsylvania, and member of the Plowshares Eight.

Glen Stassen is associate professor of Christian ethics at the Southern Baptist Theological Seminary in Louisville, Kentucky, and on the editorial staff of *The Baptist Peacemaker*.

John R. W. Stott is rector emeritus of All Souls Church, London. He is the author of many books and a contributing editor for *Sojourners* magazine.

Walter Sullivan is bishop of Richmond, Virginia.

George Zabelka is a retired diocesan priest in Lansing, Michigan. He gives workshops on nonviolence and assists in diocesan work.